Beautiful Hustle

Confessions of a "D" Girl

Beautiful Hustle
Confessions of a "D" Girl

Illustrious Empire, LLC
32455 W. 12 Mile #3086
Farmington Hills, Mi 48333
Email: Fauna@beautifulHustlethebook.com
Website:www.BeautifulHustleTheBook.com

Printed and Published in the United States of America

ISBN: 978-0-9862988-0-6

Acknowledgements

Thanks to my two loving daughters, Alexis and Fanesse whom have helped change me into the woman I am today! To the love of my *LIFE... My KING...* Jason, who is also my bestfriend and my biggest fan... I couldn't have done this without you baby! I LOVE YOU!!! Last but not Muthafuckn least... MY BFFS Rita, Tina, Candise, and Mashall, I love yall bitches!! My Boy/Bestie Fa' Life Dietrich nigga you've always been team Fauna! Cousin Freddie... you already know what it is! Anyone I didn't mention NO LOVE LOST! Got yall on the next one!!

Special thanks to *Valencia R. Williams New Lyfe Films LLC*, my sister *Fela Bey* and most importantly... *Chuck of NuManagment* for their knowledge and contributions on my journey of becoming an Author. I appreciate everything & I look forward to writing PART ll "VERY SOON!"

Dedication

I dedicate this book to my Mother and Father! My Father is the first man that I ever loved. My Mom is the first woman I admired and wanted to be JUST LIKE! Both of them are my heroes. Their arms are the first place where I felt safe and protected!

The smile that comes across my Dad's face when he sees me makes me feel so beautiful, cherished, and adored. My Dad has always been a VERY HARD WORKER. I respect him so much for working hard to provide for me and our family. It has provided me with a sense of security that has helped me in creating a fulfilling foundation for my OWN life. Don't get me wrong I have made plenty mistakes along the way I'M FAR FROM PERFECT!!

The great part is no matter how square my parents are they always ACCEPTED me for who I am. Their unconditional support & loving encouragement has always meant EVERYTHING to me! No matter how busy my Dad was he made time for me!! Seeing you at my games, recitals, graduations, and at home for dinner (every night)!! It let me know our family was a big priority in your life! Then Mom, she did all of the above & went over & beyond. She would NEVER ever miss a chance to chaperone or volunteer. Her daughters are her LIFE!! She took her "STAY AT HOME MOM" job VERY serious. Shit she deserved a raise every week if you ask me! She was my teacher. She taught me how to ride a bike, throw a ball, open a checking account, change a tire, and so much more.

To this day I still think my MOM is SUPER WOMAN! And my DAD is SUPER MAN!! I thank my dad for never cheating. His loyalty has helped me to be able to trust men even when one or two let me down, and how to be drawn to healthy, loving relationships. Most children don't get to experience a healthy household! I THANK MY MOM & DAD for that!

My Dad has always been UPFRONT & HONEST WITH ME. Never afraid to say how he feels!! I look up to him and I respect his integrity. His strong character has inspired me to value and honor myself. My parents have been my loving shoulder to cry on when my heart was broken and a hand to high five to celebrate when I achieved a dream.

They are the ONLY people I call when I need advice or when I've needed to negotiate a deal, sign a lease, or take a leap of faith. Their wisdom is GOLD to me.

I couldn't have picked a better set of parents if I could have made them from scratch!! So I dedicate this book to you!! I know I have made plenty of mistakes in my life but your support and God's love is what always gets me through!! I love you!

Prologue

Good girl gone bad, hardly. I was born a Bad Boss Bitch and from womb I was determined to live the life of the fashionably famous. From a young girl I knew I was different, I knew that eventually me breaking all rules would be a requirement to be who I wanted to be. I was destined for greatest even though it went against the morals my parents instilled in me. Their intentions were good but I didn't give a fuck about rules and regulations, I was out to get it & I did just that.

I knew my lifestyle never met my parent's approval. But the look on my Mothers face on Mother's Day somehow seemed to make it all worth it. I bought my mom a brand new car, laced it with a bow and put the keys in her mailbox. I called her phone & told her to check the mailbox for me, she didn't know I was watching from outside. She got the keys & jumped for joy. For once, I made up for making her sad.

I made millions. I traveled the world and wore the finest things. I sat court side with the stars and they know who I am. My beautiful hustle created so many opportunities. It opened doors that I never expected. I was living the life that people dreamt of, hell I am proof that dreams come true. However, I was often reminded about how I was taught better. I felt guilty for not living up to what my family thought I should be. I continued to reach my goals & fulfill my dreams and everybody around me. For Christmas I bought my parents a home that was beyond their dreams. The beautiful house was constructed around a indoor swimming pool giving it this spaceship back to the future look. I tried to heal their hurt from the life I chose by being present for birthdays, holidays and just because. Gifts, trips, the finest diamonds and furs - they were not used to this shit. For Father's Day I bought my dad's first Rolex. He deserved it. They never approved of my personal decisions, but eventually they just supported me in the best way they knew how. My parents always wanted the best for our family so it felt so good being able to do all these things. I wonder if my Dad ever realized that subliminally it was him that taught me how to make moves for the better.

1

"Let the Games Begin"

Some say growing up in Detroit is live or die. You snooze you lose. I beg to differ. The 'D' is like every other hardcore city, where hustlers hustle, killers kill and female bosses like me, live to tell their stories.

Many have said, "I think I've been here before", and sometimes I wonder the same, if I played a role in creating my own destiny. I'm not saying I'm God, don't get me confused.

I am a God fearing woman! I know without him, I would not be here today, and someone else would be telling my story. I'm just known for taking control of - let's call them "situations", for now. While most kids spent their time in La La Land hoping and wishing on a dream, I was thinking of a master plan to live mine. The beautiful hustle life began at the age of 15 and I was determined not to ever go back to the mediocre lifestyle that my parents worked so hard to give me. I yearned for more, I needed it, and I wanted it.

I had the best of both worlds, a hard working Father and a loving and devoted Mother. My older sister Fela and I were not the stereotypical kids being raised in a one parent home. We had the complete opposite. Although my Mother is white, she was not the classic white Mom you see on TV. She was no joke, did not take any BS, and made

1

sure she corrected every mispronounced word. She was a stay-at-home mom, who catered to her children and her man. As a young girl, I remember admiring my parents' relationship. Now today they are still standing strong in their 44 years of marriage. Love was always in the air, even the smallest arguments were settled without delay. They always smiled, laughed, and even joked with one another and still do. My family is one thing that I was always proud of. The love, trust and respect, was always there. However, we struggled financially like a lot of families, and *that* was the part I had a hard time relating to.

There were so many things running through my young mind. I can recall staring off into the window hoping to see a fancy car, a sharp house or someone making a fashion trend. My mind wandered beyond what society considered standard. Like most kids, I wanted the things I couldn't have, but instead of throwing a tantrum, I would make a mental note, because I knew eventually I would get it somehow, some way.

My mind developed rapidly, and my physical appearance did the same. At an early age, I would always wonder where I got my body from. I watched my Mom get dressed every day. She would prepare herself for a new day of being a wife, Mom and friend. Her choice of make-up and clothing was always to perfection, and her clothes fit her flawless body just right. I looked at her, and looked at myself and confirmed where the physical part of me came from. That alone placed me on the market a lot sooner than anticipated. I found myself always having to check a nigga for saying the wrong shit when I stepped on the scene. Once I realized that my body was a weapon and my mind was beyond my years, I knew I had what it took to get whatever I wanted. Despite growing up in a wholesome household by two great parents with strict rules, I was still determined to fulfill my own hidden agendas. Never the type to follow rules, I was extremely creative in manipulating the world that I lived in to reach the success that I always dreamed of.

By the age of 16, I was smoking weed and sneaking out the house, courtesy of my BFF Robin. I love that bitch to this very day, and she opened up a Pandora's Box just a little bit more. I had another friend Tamara, who was no help in making us do the right thing either. She, like Robin and me, wanted to live a life that our parents were never able to give us. The good life existed!

We knew it did because we saw it, and were determined to get a piece of it. Detroit's Charlie's Angels was our nickname. We ran the streets and demanded respect from every nigga that paid to play. We didn't have time for no niggas balling backwards. We were the truth, and lived every fucking day like it was our last! We had a bond, a pact to always get money, and keep it real with each other if nobody else. It was none of that fake shit you see with a lot of these so-called female friends out here. I dealt with a small circle of friends, picking them like a 4-leaf clover. It may sound a little odd but, I was a square just like my parents on one hand, but blazing up with the other. I had successfully crossed over to the good life, and loved every second of it. Hell, I had to realize, time stops for no one and neither does growth. So I was bound to shake that lame shit off sooner or later. Except sooner came faster than later!

Garcia Vegas was our thing, me and my team. Considering my lame ass, weed was my ultimate high! No

3

one could've convinced me I'd ever see the day where I would be packaging up something outside of the norm. Forcing me to step my game all the way up on that money tip. I didn't know a damn thing about hardcore drugs at that time; until I met this dude named Blue, through Robin's boo DJ. I just woke up one day and there I was stumbling up on a 40 year old man at only 16. *Maaann*, I was playing Russian roulette too, because my parents would have killed my ass if they had found that shit out!

I was having way too much fun to second-guess my decisions at the moment, besides I controlled my own destiny. It was either do or get done with this Blue dude. We took trips out of town, went on shopping sprees, and I was rocking designer shit I could barely pronounce. This cat introduced me to some glamorous shit, and made me feel like the rare gem I really was! He brought out that burning sensation that I could feel when I rode in the back seat of the family car. The same feeling I got when I realized that not everybody struggled, there was a good life and brighter days. One dose of that life and I was too far gone. At that point I didn't really give a fuck about what my Mom and Dad thought. I was living the life! I'm talking Versace, Coogi, and Gators in every style and color. I mean, dude had me up in Canada on some gangsta shit! He took me to this warehouse where I saw live animals running around in cages awaiting their fate to a balling ass nigga, who sat back picking out which one of the animals he wanted to wear on his and his bitches back. Now that was some real custom shit. I'm talking quality shit like minks and rich fur textures. Straight glamour shit!

I was so overwhelmed with minks, designer clothing and diamonds; that by the time I was introduced to packing up heroin in Tops papers and aluminum foil for dude, I was intrigued to learn even more. He fed the burning sensation that lived in my body before I knew what it was. He catered to my needs and wants like not even my parents could. Watching him move and shake made me rattle and roll! It was more exciting than discouraging. Sounds crazy, I know but it was the beginning of a story that never ended. I'm talking about more money than a pretty bitch from the streets of Detroit could count, and more dope than Tony Montana could snort up his nose!

Now you know with all this comes some excessive ass drama... To make all that money so easily was like landing a record deal. And to think, the only thing I saw growing up, was a Mom with strong values, solid family structure in our household, and a Dad that worked extra hard to get us by.

All that was cool, but what Blue did was SO EASY!!! I was making $500-$600 a day packaging up dope minus the cost of putting in 6-8 hours straight doing the shit! To me it was easy money! I even packaged the shit at home, telling my parents I was making hair papers for my friend's hair salon and they never questioned it, why would they? They raised me to know better but this life was too good! Imagine a 16 year old with thousands of dollars buying up all kinds of shit. Before I knew it I was one of the youngest boss ladies on Detroit's west side.

2

"Gangsta Love"

It was just another day on my grind. I had lost track of time packing heroin for hours with my man Blue and his crew. He loved to show me off to all his friends, and this particular day was no different from any other. While in the midst of my hustle, this big handsome dude walks in and had the prettiest smile, along with the best mannerisms I'd ever seen. This man was like a big teddy bear. He introduced himself.

"Hello beautiful, my name is Butch." He said, while leaning over and kissing my hand. I have to admit, I thought that was a bit extra, but he made me feel like a lady.

Although we were packing shit up and trying to get all the work we had in front of us under wraps, his conversation was very interesting. So much that I kind of pushed things aside and paid special attention to him. We sat at the table for what seemed like hours, talking about everything from religion to politics. This man was smart, and I was really into his philosophical demeanor. I was intrigued because he was something different, and I liked different.

I didn't know much about his history; in fact this was my first encounter with this gentleman. It wasn't until Blue broke everything down about him that made me realize I had officially come in contact with a real

American Gangsta. I was deeply impressed. Butch was this professional dude that made me feel a little uneasy sitting at a table filled with dope. I had some mixed emotions about that shit.

Here I was, this beautiful young chick moving large sums of dope right before his eyes, while he sat across from me kicking it about politics and other shit. This was one of the many reasons why I wanted to know what kind of business he was in. Hell, he was sitting across from me with over $100,000 worth of dope scattered across the table like a median in the highway, I really just wanted to find out whatever I could about this "Mr. Jones."

Blue simply said,

"Baby-Girl, this dude is an incredible book writer, on some real shit, and I'm a bring you his book tomorrow. I got one at the crib!"

"Book writer, huh?" I thought to myself, "Now I get it! That's why he's so smart."

When Blue brought me his book I looked like a kid sitting at the Christmas tree on Christmas morning, waiting to open that one special gift.

"Here you go, Ma," Blue said as he tossed the book across the room to me. I flipped it around, looking over the front and back cover.

"YBI? Damn. You mean this whole time I've been talking to BUTCH JONES?!" I sounded like a groupie backstage at a Tupac concert, but I didn't give a fuck.

"You never know who yo' boy got stuffed in his back pocket. I got friends baby, and they're not just your average muthafuckas you see in your everyday world. These are your balling-ass-well-respected-in-the-streets muthafuckas the average nigga can't sit in the same room with." Blue said leaning down in the refrigerator pulling out a pitcher of Kool-Aid I just made.

That nigga loved him some Fauna sweet ass Kool-Aid, grape to be exact.

"Your teeth gon' be rotten from drinking that sweet shit all the time baby. If you ain't gobbling down that Kool-Aid like you just ran a marathon. Yo' ass eating up bags of candy just fucking up yo' grill!" I teased him.

He looked at me and smiled. That's how the nigga got the pussy in the first place, low key. Blue had a white lineup from God! Not many men I come across have a grill that was as immaculate as his! I swear if he loses one tooth, especially one in his front row, I would leave his ass where he stood. I was funny like that. It didn't take much to turn me off, but it took a lot to turn me on. I dove into the YBI book. It was the first gangster novel I read, so to get my own, signed copy from the man himself, made a bitch feel honored. I fingered through it, page after page, and found myself falling in love with not only his writing but also his personal swag! I just couldn't believe this teddy bear was a straight up gangster. Damn...

It was another day of flipping, stuffing and bagging up work. My ass barely got any sleep from staying up late the night before reading Teddy Bear's (Butch Jones) book all damn night. I found my mind transforming the words in the book, to actual images and scenes. The money, the fast cars and designer clothes intrigued me. It was definitely a page-turner. I left it on my nightstand and tried to focus my attention back on my money. Everything was going smooth for a minute, to the point where I became relaxed. Money was coming in and dope was going out. It was like an assembly line. This was my 9 to 9. I moved to my Nana's house with my sister Fela, where I had more leeway in moving shit smoothly without the threat of being caught up by my parents. Although I wanted to believe I had control over everything, fate did not spare me. Just thinking back on it gives me the chills. I am always ready and prepared for whatever but this day, Moms had one up on me.

What's that saying? –"What you do in the dark comes to light?"

Well, I got my ass lit up when my Mom crept up on me at one of the worst times ever! Somewhat like the scene from my favorite movie, "Notorious", about rapper Biggie Smalls. Angela Bassett, who played Biggie's mom, much like my Mom was, always cleaning and snooping. Ms. Wallace thought what was really cocaine hidden under his bed, was leftover potato residue and tossed it in the trash! The only difference between his story and mine, was that the dope my Mom tossed off the table was Blue's not mine! The $80,000 worth of work that graced my table belonged to someone else! My heart raced, my mind went faster, and my limbs began to shake. The look on Moms face when she walked in on us was priceless as she flipped the table over, and the dope that sat like a pile of dust on the table went flying in the air like a smoke cloud. Poof! Just like that, my life flashed before my eyes. No ass-whooping could snap me out of the zone I was in. I couldn't utter a word. I didn't even notice her throwing everyone out! That's how fucked up I was behind that shit!

How was I going to explain this to Blue? There is no way I could repay him, I mean I had some bread, but not that damn much. What should I say? How will he react? At this age, most girls worst fear is an ass woopin... Damn that ass woopin! I didn't wanna be found dead in the Detroit

9

River with cement on my feet! Yeah I may be a pretty bitch, but I am far from dumb. Even the movies show you what happens when you fuck up the money or the work.

"What the fuck have I gotten myself into?" I questioned myself as I slid to the floor. My Mother towering over me pointing her finger in my face, cussing and even her tears couldn't break the trance I was in. We're talking a bird of raw, uncut, pure shit totaling over eighty racks in the streets! The only thing going through my head while getting my ass chewed and glued was, 'That shit was not coming out of the carpet... damn Ma.'

I told both my best friends what happened, just in case my ass came up missing. I went to Blue shortly after, to see what else fate had in store for me. I am a bad bitch to the core, and decided to be honest and admit that I had fucked up bad! Luckily, Blue understood the situation, appreciated my honesty and admired how loyal I was. Part of me felt like he already knew and was waiting for me to come to him. I began to wonder who could have told him. Was it somebody that my Moms kicked out? They didn't see anything though, because they ran out soon as she bust in the room. Maybe they heard her yelling and assumed, I don't know. All I do know is, I only told two people and I know my girls wouldn't cross me... At least I prayed they wouldn't. Nevertheless, my ass is alive and my Moms always said the truth will set you free. I was free and back to work. Blue complemented my work ethic as he put his hand on my shoulder and whispered in my ear "It's nothing to a boss baby". His hand gently swept my hair off my neck as he walked away.

3

"Weak for Fauna"

Although I was basically living at my Nana's house, my parents forbid me to ever see him again. Now, anyone who knows me knows damn well I wasn't one to follow the rules. I just became more creative with the moves I made when it came to doing whatever the fuck I wanted to. Having this thing for older men was something I had grown accustomed to. I needed something to do after getting caught up. My parents had been ridin' my heels after the raid my Mom did at my Nana's house, so I had to press pause on my beautiful hustle, and even Blue for that matter. The whole family was tripping. Forcing me to focus my attention back on my education, and I did just that, at least long enough for them to ease up. It was only a matter of time before the ball was back in my court, and I was back to doing what I wanted to do, just slicker. Time was of the essence, and it was time for me to press play again.

I was feeding the indescribable sensation that filled my belly, even as a young girl. I never had a name for it and it seemed as if nobody felt this way but me. It was something my body yearned for me to feed, although I knew many of the things I did to tickle my palette left a seriously bad taste in my parents' mouth. I no longer sought after their approval. I was introduced to a world that fed my sensations. I tried my best to stay focused on my education but at this point age was just a number, and I was in pursuit of my own happiness. It was my way or no way, even in school.

I was there for my education, but I had set my eyes on another prize. Mr. B, who was my teachers' fine ass! I couldn't stop staring at him, discreetly tho', at least I thought I was. There was definitely no way in this world I was going to let a brotha know I was feeling him.

I always remember the words *"The one who loves the least, controls the Relationship."*

My Nana always said that. So, I kept that in mind and knew I had to protect myself going in. It was the only way to maintain control once the trap was set. Just like a fly caught in my web, once you're in, you're in and there is no turning back. This man could lose everything; his job, his career and even his family, but I knew it wouldn't be long before he would risk all of those things for the one thing he craved, me.

Mr. B was a sexy ass older man, and you know what they say about older men. The head and dick game is off the chain! Though older men are a little more seasoned than we are; what any of them that crossed my path didn't know is that I've been here before, and knew how to play the game. That was my little secret. So even if these older John Doe's have been around longer than us, studying our breed, trying to understand our sexual anatomy, and then how to mentally control us – the shit they would try to run on my young ass gets turned around and used against their old ass - LOL! I was a mastermind of all men.

So back to Mr. B… when I was in his class he would give me that look. You know the one that screamed out, *"Damn, I want that pussy!"* LOL! It was only shortly after that, when I started putting my manipulation plan in motion.

One day I asked him for a pass to my next class because I was late. Of course he obliged, and it wasn't long after before he was inviting me into his *private* office that was in the back of his classroom. I couldn't help but notice how he would watch my ass as I walked past him. He pretended to be busy checking papers or whatever it was he did, but he kept his eye on me. The crush I had on him was just as obvious as the one he had on me, but there were huge risk factors and we both knew. I mean who were we kidding? What we had was an undeniable attraction and we would certainly be breaking all the rules, but we didn't let that stop us. Within a couple weeks, we were hooking up on his lunch breaks during school hours and having the most intense sex that was far from your typical teacher student relationship. Despite the fact that I was skating on thin ice by fucking around with an authority figure, it was the threat itself that made it even more of a challenge, and actually what I loved the most. The secrecy, the risk and the intensity of it all fed that undesirable burning sensation that lived within me. Real talk… that creeping around shit made my pussy throb.

I remember how nervous he was the very first time we hooked up on some gettin-it-in shit. I knew this night in particular, by it being our first time, was going to be all about turning his old ass out and showing him what I was about. Although he looked like he has had some interesting pussy in his days, the fact of the matter was he hadn't had THIS pussy, and that changed things all together. He had no idea what this lil school girl had in store for him.

We met up downtown after hours at the Westin Hotel, inside the Renaissance Center. The Westin is now the Marriott Hotel and the Renaissance Center is currently owned by General Motors. That fact comes as a shock to many of us because the Renaissance has been an icon to Detroiters for as long as I could remember. When you see the Renaissance Center you know its Detroit. The layout is still the same but the hotel and some of the architectural designs are different. Everything was and still is very nice and upscale. I felt very special that Mr. B chose this place for our first meet up spot. I guess I wasn't really expecting a school teacher to have elaborate taste in locations for making love, so I was pretty impressed. I like nice shit, and I'm sure he probably noticed that. I love a man that pays attention.

On his salary I expected mediocre, like perhaps we would have ended up at some cheap little BS spot similar to the Grand Marquise Hotel across from Motown Records off Grand Boulevard. But I guess I under estimated this man, which made fucking him at that point even easier.

"Where you at baby?" I asked seductively over the phone as I waited naked laying across a king sized bed that sat up on a pedestal in a huge executive suite, looking over a nice spread of the Detroit River and Canada. The sun had just gone down and the water sparkled. I gazed out the window inhaling the feeling and waiting for the moment he walks through the door. I gently pulled on my nipples arousing myself preparing for this official encounter. He had arranged this particular room for such a special occasion. We spent time together alone before, but never a good enough amount of time for me to make him my victim. Tonight he will see what little ole me has to offer. I was prepared to fulfill his every need.

I was glad I made it there before him. That gave me just enough time to set my plan in motion and get a feel for my surroundings. It was a beautiful room and I wanted to make sure everything lined up the way I wanted it to.

"I'm pulling up to valet right now. You there?" He said in that deep voice that made my pussy flutter,

"*Mmmhumm*. Been here waiting on yo' ass." I purred looking up at the ceiling that displayed a hand crafted 'W' reflecting down at me. This is the life, I thought to myself.

Honestly, the set up had me wet up, and I was more than ready for this night to begin. I went through a lot to stay out without all the interrogating from my parents. Humph, the dick better be on point or I will leave his ass in this big ole nice room never to be heard from again!! I pondered on what he had planned for me, reevaluated the things I had in store for him and waited a little longer. The anticipation made the clock move slower.

I was getting bored waiting, so I slid my hand under the pillow where I put my vibrator. I had conveniently named it Tyson Beckford. I brought it with me just in case I needed a little help getting my nut. I heard good and bad stories about sex with older men therefore, I knew without a doubt I was gonna make him get his, but I would be a fool not to get mine. I pulled out Tyson to entertain myself while I anxiously waited for him. Spreading my legs apart gracing my finger across my tongue to add to the juice that was already flowing from my pussy simply from the thought of how my night would begin. I rubbed my fat throbbing piece of pink skin that stood out like one of the world's most expensive pearls and lubricated it in a circular motion.

"*Ooooooh* shit... yes that's it." I moaned and caressed that cherry as it began to swell up.

It was about ready for Tyson. Not taking any attention away from an already in motion rhythm I had going on, rotating my hips in sync with my finger I was only a few minutes away from my orgasm without using Tyson at all, "*Ooooooooh* Damn!" I closed my eyes and moaned as I reached over my head to feel for my toy. Before I could grab it to finish where I started...

"Looking for this?" Mr. B said standing beside the bed butt ass naked with a monster hard dick damn near plucking out my right eye! I sat up grabbing a sheet, kind of embarrassed at him sneaking up on me like that!

"How did you...?" I nervously made an attempt to try and figure out how his ass got into the room, got undressed and was actually standing over me for God knows how long looking like the actor *Laz Alonso*! This was the best way to describe him, with his to-die-for smile watching my horny ass! I was a little embarrassed but I was ready.

"*Shhhhh...*" He seductively responded with his finger over his lips, utilizing his left hand and holding his dick in the right. I just stared up at his muscular body, meeting him eye to eye, following his every demand as he snatched the sheet off while crawling onto the bed wrapping his hand around my ponytail.

'Take that shit nigga...,' my thoughts crooned.

He took a nice but gentle hold, kneeling down and placing his soft wet tongue in my mouth. Not only did he smell good as fuck, but he kissed me in a way I had never,

16

and I mean *never been* kissed before. That nigga was for sho' a good kissah! I was all in. I felt like he had me under his spell right then, as he gently caressed my nipples that were even harder than they were when I was touching myself!

He completely took over and came in where I left off. He laid me back on the bed and released his hold on my hair. He needed the support of both hands to stabilize me in the position he needed me in, to do what he wanted to do. I was on my back and he slid his wet tongue down to my nipples taking them whole in his mouth like sweet plums handpicked from the Whole Foods Market. I moaned from the pleasurable feelings as I received his every move. Taking both of my breasts into his strong hands, pulling them into each other as he licked them simultaneously, lubricating them with his warm saliva. I swear on everything it was the best nipple-tit massage I had ever had in my life! I was so ready for some dick inside me at that moment, but he obviously had something else in mind so I had to find some patience and roll with the plan.

Before I could open my eyes to see what was next in line, he was making his way down to my apple tree, plunging his tongue inside me like he was searching for a hidden treasure. I had never felt a tongue that had the potential to work just as good as a dick. That muthafucka fell so deep into my tight hole I subconsciously threw my legs up spreading my lips apart with my two index fingers giving him all the leeway he needed to find whatever he was looking for. That shit right there nigga, was righteous! I threw that pussy into his face like one of *Mayweather's* punches – you would of thought I had a 50 Cent beef with his ass. With the smacking noises from all the juices that were pouring into his face, I had to check his pulse to make sure I hadn't drowned his ass. I was in a zone! Out of nowhere this strong muthafucka flipped me some kind of way where I ended up on top of his face riding the shit out of it. It didn't take long before the gates of heaven opened, and an orgasm that I had been patiently waiting on came pouring out.

I screamed out in this hard cry of ecstasy from that deep sensation he had unlocked in me. Climbing off his face, body still in shivers, he looked at me and winked, folded his hands behind his head and smiled.

"What you smiling at?" I said reaching for a half towel on the nightstand.

"You're so pretty, Fauna."

"Is that right?" I made an attempt to wipe my juices that was all over his face off and he said,

"Naw, ladies first," as he moved my hand away.

"Huh?" I said confused.

"You can handle yours first baby, then you can wipe my face for me."

"You so nasty, Mr. B." I said grinning.

"You haven't seen what nasty is yet," he responded with an evil grin.

I knew then, the night was far from over. I followed his wishes, wiping all that wet shit from between my ass then reusing the same towel to wipe his face. Now that was a little much, but after I cleaned his face off we were back up and running!

I hummed on his balls that smelled like the scent of Coast soap and used my tongue to outline any and every area around his dick to make his ass moan like a bitch! At one point I thought the nigga was putting on an act, but when his nut was ready to crack that shit came pouring and squirting out so fast it damn near chocked my ass to death. The salty taste of his nut was so intense it forced my face to frown up, but I fucking love the taste of that shit cuz I'm freaky as hell, and I want to have total control over the dick by the time that nigga raise up.

"Whose dick is this?" I said aggressively with his dick in my hand.

"You already know... Yours Fauna" He confirmed.

I could tell this stone cold freak I was laying next to wanted to see what level of freakiness I was on. Hoping I would go as far as to gargle or blow bubbles with his nut LOL! I knew then I had to switch up on em' in order to get on his level. I was doing some things to him that made his eyes damn near pop out of his head. I climbed on top of him as I sat my naked ass comfortably on his chest making my pussy throb as he stared up at me finding everything I was doing amusing. When we finished, we laid there in what seemed like a coma.

"Damn that shit was good!" He confessed.

"Yea it was... Do you mind?" I pulled out my meds rolling up preparing to smoke.

"They say we're not supposed to smoke in these rooms but after all that, they can keep my fucking deposit! Light that shit up!"

"Yea right Mr. B... You don't smoke." I teased firing up.

"I do now," he laughed.

It was right then when I knew Fauna was in the lead as I could hear the audience roar! The burning sensation in my belly was fulfilled. Damn this is what I been needing in my life and didn't even know it. I took a turn off the path

19

society designed for me, and decided to live life by my own rules. This night with Mr. B was my reward for being me. When he asked me did I have a boyfriend, of course I said no, and went on to tell him that I had just broken something off because my parents thought the guy I was with was too old for me. I think me telling him this secretly gave him the green light that age was nothing but a number in my eyes. It was after that when everything went from school to a full-blown relationship.

Yea, he was married; but ask me, did I care? I felt very little emotion about that shit. He was my reward remember. So when he went into this spiel about being unhappily married, though I believed him, I really didn't give a fuck fa'real! I watch niggas like him through my 3rd eye very closely. Sometimes they shift mental gears on you so fast that if you're not careful, you'll get caught up in their transmission. But I liked Mr. B tho'. I had to admit, our relationship was different than the norm, besides our age difference of course. But almost like a flirty relationship. I was young, hot and damn near every man's fantasy. So I could only imagine what the wife was going through after coming face to face with her competition. Shit got real then.

I saw the infamous wife for the first time when she ran up on Mr. B's truck while we sat talking one day. She had his two younger sons in the car with her, yelling out,

"LOOK AT YOUR DADDY HE AINT SHIT!"

She even tried to get some heart and swing on me. I leaned back as I felt the wind from her swing blow past my face. I cut my eye at her then cut my eye at Mr. B. He already knew if I got out that car it would be the day her sons would see her get that ass whooped, so I held my composure and Mr. B pulled off trying to explain to make me feel better. I knew then everything he worked so hard for was going to soon come to a screeching stop. Oh well, that was the price you paid when fucking with a boss bitch like me! It's a throw of the dice. Either you feed what fuels you or you make it starve. I chose to feed mine by any means necessary. If I want it I'll go after it & I'll get it. Period! I am a boss.

That next day his wife was calling up to the school telling everything she knew about us. There's a saying;

"It ain't what you know, but it's what you can prove."

Well, unbeknownst to me, this bitch had recorded phone conversations of me and him during the wee hours of the night and hired a private investigator. They even had pictures and shit. Not to mention the school was able to roll back some camera footage and saw my ass driving his whip! It was downhill from there. Our fun had come to an end. His weakness for me destroyed everything he worked for.

All my shopping sprees, smoking blunts after school with him and my BFF Robin, and pushing his brand new Navigator was a wrap! His career plunged like bad stock. Although I was really feeling him, I wasn't ready for something long-term. When the question of me and him living together came up, I knew it wasn't a chance in hell; I had too much living to do. Hell he was just a part of the feast needed to feed the burning sensation that I craved more than him. Then one day I got a disturbing phone call from his wife while he supposedly sat there, telling me my relationship with him was over. I admitted, my feelings were kind of hurt, but I knew it was more to the story. He had *just* come to me with the idea of us living together. I knew it was something he had to do to save the things that sustained our relationship.

Back to reality! Back to school meant facing my fate. All the gossip was *horrible*. I didn't even wanna go back to that shit. My sister Fela even tried to go up to Oak Park High and talk to them. She told them she was the one who dated him. They bombarded her with questions regarding the green Navigator that I was driving, and she could easily defend that because she had a dark blue one. But it was just crazy, they had so much evidence of me and him together; they weren't buying into it no matter what she said. My sister always had my back no matter how wrong I was and even when I didn't take her advice. Good bad happy or sad we have our differences but when the cookie crumbles we have each other.

At this point I was disgusted and done. Mr. B was fired and banned from working in any school district period! Playtime was over! It was then when I realized I could possibly have done the move-in thing with him. Basically to piss his wife off even more, being that I was the bitch that had what she used to have and now she wanted it back! But honestly, she just wasn't enough of a challenge for me and neither was he. He filled my sensation for that moment but settling down and moving in was not a part of my destiny or any parts of my future. I came to realize that the mere thought of settling down at the age of 17, and not being able to date other people slapped me in the face hard. My ass woke up real quick!

I'm not gon' front, I had feelings for Mr. B, deep feelings and I didn't want to hurt him too bad. I played with the idea of us in this fairytale relationship for some time but deep inside we both knew it would never manifest. I searched for other things to feed that burning sensation that fed my drive and determination. I knew I needed excitement, money, cars and clothes. I needed something and someone who wanted to live like I wanted to live, saw things how I saw them and was willing to get it by any means necessary. I closed the chapter titled "Mr. B" and opened a new chapter dedicated to my adventures with some fly "D" boys. How was he not enough anymore? I questioned myself. Will these urges ever be satisfied and go away? All of a sudden this proper man, this teacher, wasn't so attractive. We weren't having as much fun as I did with the "D" boys and he was starting to get overly jealous. So I slowly but surely started backing out of that relationship. Last I heard Mr. B was broke and getting high. *Life...*

4

"neXt"

On to the next... Time stops for no one. Here I am 18, and although I didn't graduate, I was determined to make a future for myself. I had stopped going to school all together. I was tired of hearing about me and Mr. B. It was no longer cute and I was embarrassed by it. The jokes, sarcasm and bold looks from other teachers were just too much for me. I'm not soft, far from it, but I also knew that I didn't have to endure that mess. It was back to reality and back to being slick to make things happen my way. My parents thought I never missed a day of school. My Mom would drop me off for school in the morning at the front door every day. Little did she know I was right out the back door runnin the streets and smokin non-stop with Robin the whole school day until I was supposed to be home. I was back on the prowl. Living life as I see fit with no regard.

In an attempt to do something that met my parents' approval, I ended up with a job at Ford Motor Credit making a decent salary. The transition from street money to legit money was a major struggle for me, but I had to start somewhere. I knew I had to generate some income for myself. I wasn't the type to rely on others to keep my pockets fat. Don't get me wrong tho', I love being catered to, but most importantly, I am a self-made bitch who will always make sure I have the best of the best. That being said, I'm always keeping my eyes open for volunteers who want to invest in the Fauna Bank & Trust.

On my lunch break with my BFF Robin at S&C's, one of our favorite restaurants since we were 16, we were hungry as hell and had very little time to stick and move. Who did I see? This fine ass chocolate dude surrounded by what appeared to be his boys laughing and joking around, just enjoying life. It was the kind of energy I loved to see when I'm in the same room with men. I was drawn to their conversation. These cats really appeared to be living in the moment. It was alluring.

I found myself giggling under my breath and I didn't even know what the hell I was giggling at. It was one of those self-conscious moves. The crazy thing was I couldn't keep my eyes off Mr. Chocolate Sensation. This man had the sexiest smile. Knowing how I was about teeth... white straight teeth to be exact. He had my full attention off the rip!

The mystery man and his boys were dressed nice on this cold Detroit day. The fact that Mr. Chocolate Sensation was wearing one of the baddest minks I had seen since my Canadian trip I took a few months ago to the animal slaughterhouse, had me intrigued.

"Damn bitch!" Robin shoved me damn near forcing me to spill my drink!

"Whaaat! You almost made me spill this drink on my blouse hoe!"

"That may have been the only thing that would snap you the fuck out of that trance you was just in looking over at that black Negro!" She giggled, staring over in the same direction I was.

"You obviously see something you like over there too bitch!" I said.

"Tssst... Fauna please! I gotta man, remember?" She rolled her eyes.

"Since when did that make a difference?" I teased.

"I don't cheat bitch." She stared at me.

"Might I remind you that I am your best friend that knows e-v-e-r-y-t-h-i-n-g about you, hoe." I took a bite of my sandwich and wiped the sides of my lips.

"You got nothing on me." She teased.

We continued going back and forth, a pretty normal thing with us. We didn't even notice that we were now being checked out by the guys we had just been scoping with our radars.

Before I could even take notice, he sent a waitress I was very familiar with named Stella over to pay our bill. I was kinda impressed by that. I kept it cool though, and looked over giving him one of those head nods. He smiled and I turned my attention back to my silly ass friend who couldn't wait to make another sarcastic comment.

"So is this the next victim or volunteer?" She sipped her drink and giggled.

"I don't know what you're talking about. Come on, let's go, I got to get back to work before they dock my ass." I stood up, and gathered my things to leave. Before I could head toward the door, he was on my heels.

Approaching calmly, his cologne graced my nose and before he could say a word I was under his spell.

"My name is Will." His deep voice with that smile made my knees buckle. The good thing about it was, he couldn't tell I was nervous. I had become creative when it came to hiding my emotions. I learned that the hard way.

I turned and met him face-to-face stuck in amazement on how fine this muthafucka was to look at and responded,

"I'm Fauna and this is my girl…"

Before I could roll her name off my tongue her crazy outspoken ass responded with,

"Robin, her *best* friend." she clarified.

She stared at him for 2 seconds, looked around him, then at his two friends behind him.

"Who are these two clowns?" Robin gestured her index finger between the two guys accompanying dude embarrassing the shit out of me and continued, "Your bodyguards?" I was done.

"Excuse me for a minute." I said to him. "Robin." I playfully stepped in between them two with my back turned to him. "Don't you have somewhere you need to be?" I mumbled to her.

"Nope." She popped her lips.

Robin was one of those sister-like friends that were always trying to oversee shit. I love her to death and I know she wants the best for me, but damn she was like Solange before we ever even heard of Beyonce. Thinking about that crazy shit with Jay-Z and Beyonce's sister reminded me a lot of how Robin was about me. She will clock out on a nigga so fast over me, I swear. One wrong move, one wrong word and it's their ass without notice.

"Excuse my friend, she's… He cut me off attempting to finish my sentence.

"…making sure you're in good hands, which I want to assure you, you would be, if a brotha can get in line…which I'm sure the waiting list to take you out is long."

"That was so fuckn' corny." Robin replied from a distance.

I looked at her with my mouth open and gave her this grim eye which meant she had better chill out with all that silly shit she was on. I was feeling dude and she was not making this connection easy for me.

Robin walked outside to her car and I turned my attention back to him and his friends who thought it was funny.

"Sorry about that y'all." I tried to explain

"You don't have to be sorry, Ma. You should see how these niggas act when people approach me in an open setting." He looked back over his shoulder pointing at his boys he came with.

They both made humorous jokes at his comment, and I couldn't help but laugh as we made our way outside. Robin had left which meant the bitch had an attitude, but, I was used to it. She loved attention, especially from me, so I would catch up to her later. We had a bond that was the closes thing to being blood. I had only a few minutes to wrap this conversation up, with the hopes of locking in something between the two of us before the end of my 45-minute break. Shit better had been worth it too!

"Where you on your way to on this cold day in the D?" He said as his friends walked away which I assumed meant they went to get his whip.

I quickly remembered when I was going back and forth with Robin, I noticed him passing one of them his keys. That was one thing about me, I learned at an early age. You got to have eyes on the sides and in the back of your head when dealing with the streets, period. You never know what fool may try you out here. One step ahead

28

of the game is what came natural to me after being around so many different kinds of people in my past and present life.

"A sista gotta get back to work!" I said in a shivery tone.

Anyone that has been to Detroit knows how cold it can get up in this bitch and this day in particular was one of the coldest.

"What nigga got yo' fine ass out here working?" He asked following me over to my car.

During this time I was driving my lil Ford Focus I just bought. I thought nothing of it and didn't even feel the need to respond to his comment. I hit the alarm keypad button to unlock my doors to get in. It Drew his attention and he started looking at my car with his face twisted up as if he couldn't believe I was driving a standard vehicle. I felt kinda uncomfortable at that point, after turning my car and the heat on.

I asked,

"What's wrong?" Looking up at him from my driver's seat, as he stood by my window.

"Yo man got you drivin' this baby?" He said with his nose turned up.

"No Hun, I got myself drivin' in this!" I said with confidence.

"You see, this is why you need a man like me. You too fucking pretty to be ridin' in this baby-girl!" He said while looking down the street watching a vehicle slowly pull up.

Right then his boys pulled up in a new big body Benz which was pretty popular back then for ballers like him to have. That was our way of knowing who had what. Lucky for my observant ass I knew who the owner was of the car before game was ever ran on me. Remember, I saw him toss his boys the keys to the car! Boom! I had to be careful when it came to some of these perped-out guys in Detroit. It's pretty common for a dude to whip up on a female in some sweet shit that belongs to either his chick, his boy or even worse... his Moms! And I can't stand a Momma's boy! They whine too damn much for me!

I was geeked about my little Ford Focus, I wasn't thinking about what he said. The fact that it was brand fucking new and it was mine was enough for me. After he reached deep in his pocket and pulled out a wad of cash, I was all in any way! He ran me $500 to go shopping and buy myself something cute to wear, and then meet up with him later! At first he had my interest, but after the money gesture, dude had my full attention. I wanted to go back to work and yell,

"I quit, fuck y'all!" But I snapped back and realized my car note was due. That $500 was unexpected and not coming weekly. My time was up and I had to get back to work.

Before pulling off and heading back to work, we made the plan for me to grab something cute and meet up with him at this club in downtown Detroit called *Legends*. I was all smiles, inside of course! He knew he had a potential compatible female player, and that may have been who he had been looking for all his life. But no one in a million years could have told me at that very moment, Mr. Chocolate Sensation would be the man I would later marry.

5

"A Grain of Salt"

I love to shop for the best, especially when it's at someone else's expense. There's not a designer out there that doesn't look hot on me. I have a genuine love for fashion. So, finding something nice to rock for Mr. Chocolate Sensation wasn't a challenge for me at all. I hustled to the mall to find something that will make Mr. Chocolate Sensation's mouth drop to the floor.

"I'm a bad bitch", I said to myself as I mixed and matched pieces to make my outfit complete. I gaze in the mirror to imagine how each piece will flatter my nice curves. People tell me all the time how gorgeous I am, and how I should have pursued something in the beauty or fashion field. Little do they know, I took full advantage of what I was blessed with. I might not have done it as a model, a video vixen, or a beauty pageant winner, but I honestly know in a lot of cases, my looks have worked to my advantage. I know I sound a little arrogant right now, but that's not who I am. I am just being honest.

You got some chicks out there that were blessed like me and throw it in the not-so-pretty bitch's face to make them feel more secure. Those bitches got personal problems. Your self-esteem should not be determined by putting someone else down. I believe that everybody is

31

beautiful in their own way. I am not insecure by far, and I got a lot of love for women. All types of women, it doesn't matter if you're beautiful or butt-ass ugly, it's the inner beauty that really counts. I've seen many chicks lock down some balling ass dudes... *T.I.* and *Tiny* for one! Me personally, I think Tiny is a'ight. She ain't oogly-ugly and she seems to be a loving and caring person. But honestly no one could have EVER told me she would have locked down one of the hardest rappers in the south!

Society has led us, including myself, to believe he should be with some exotic chick. Not to mention ever since Rubber band man TIP was my man in my head. Unfortunately society has these predetermined rules based on appearance alone and unfortunately some people don't benefit from it. The brains are more important than beauty or booty. However there are a few women like me who are blessed with the 3 B's. I use all three at the same damn time whenever I feel it will benefit me. God blessed me with Brains, Beauty and Booty so I may as well use it.

Anyhow, out here in these streets I would cross many paths with ugly ass chicks with fine ass men or vice versa!

I'd ask,

"How the fuck did that fat ass bitch get that rich ass nigga?" Or, *"I know damn well he not fucking her?"* and these be some proud ass men with these *Whoopi Goldberg* looking-ass-bitches on their arm. It had to be real love or proven loyalty.

I knew it had to be something that the eye could not possibly see. I had to know what it was... What could it be?

There was this not-so-pretty older chick that stayed on my block I used to look up to, who had 4 kids by this millionaire.

She told me one day,

"Fauna, you only have half of what these men out here are looking for in a woman which means the other half will be gotten somewhere else."

I looked at her confused. Hell, I was only 11 years old at the time and I would come over to hang out with her daughter Ariel after school pretty often. Though I didn't care too much for her fat ass daughter that always used to be eating up my candy and shit, but I was intrigued with her Mom, and how she was living. She was everything I aspired to be when I grew up. The family life, the paid husband, the glamorous life, the whole damn dream! This is what I consciously sought after.

I was a little lost for words after her comment at first, because I didn't understand where she was going with the conversation. I was only 11 years old, but I was smart enough to pretty much understand what she was getting at. She knew I was more mature than the average mostly because of the way I acted around her daughter during my visits.

"What do you mean by half, Mrs. King?" I stared up at her as she stood over me stirring cake mix in a bowl waiting to receive this knowledge that I would carry with me forever.

"You're very pretty, but pretty don't hold down the relationship with your man honey. Pretty can get you fucked, knocked up on welfare and broke."

"So are you saying because I'm pretty I won't have what you have?" I asked confused.

33

"Have what I have?" She smiled, put the bowl down and leaned back on her counter with her arms folded looking down into my eyes intensely. I could tell right then that there were so many things she wanted to say. Experiences she wanted to share but she knew my young mind could not grasp it all, just yet.

I replied,

"Yea, what you have. I want to live like this one day, Mrs. King."

"Oh do you now?" she responded.

I nodded my head as I looked around her huge kitchen with the skylight that sat in the center of her ceiling.

"Then you have to be prepared to endure all the pain that comes with having this life. You cannot care about shit he does. That means who he's fucking, the nights he doesn't come home. You have to love him as a human being, not as a man, and that my little princess is how you win. The only reason why I have what I have is not really about the win, it was the fact that I made it okay to lose. I lost my self –respect, the value of love and simply settled for everything this life came with. Now, do you think you can handle that Fauna?"

"Ummm, I guess so."

"WRONG ANSWER FAUNA!" Her loud and unexpected response made me jump.

I was in the hot seat unprepared for the realness that I seemingly brought upon myself.

"It's all or nothing, no in between. Now I'm going to ask you again. Can you handle the truth about the lies many of these men live? No matter how horrible, how disrespectful? Can you still have his dinner hot and ready when he gets home? Can you have his bath water running and massage his back after he stayed out 2 or 3 nights and walked through that door like he had just got in from a long day at work? Can you Fauna?" Her questions coming at me like bullets from an AK. Fast, strong and piercing. "Can you handle the truth about his lies?" She looked at me with both pain and strength.

I just stared up at her receiving everything she just said, taking it with a grain of salt and innocently responded with,

"I can't answer that right now," and started to walk away.

She looked at me and laughed, picked up her bowl, turned her back to me and started pouring it in the cake pan. She never looked back at me, and said,

"Ariel is in her room."

I walked away hoping she wasn't upset with me for not giving her a straight answer right then. I felt so much pressure from her, although I understood her every word. I just couldn't give her an answer then, and that conversation is still stuck in my head till this very day.

6

"First Love"

Legends night club was the hangout spot downtown where everybody that was somebody, showed up and blowed up. It was always bottles poppin' and asses droppin', it was a nice night and a big turnout. Detroit nightlife is the best. Like my Mother, I always took pride in my appearance. I always felt like I was going on an audition and had only one time to shine. Nothing was going to stop me from landing the role for the lead lady. There was definitely competition in the building, but I wasn't discouraged at all. I had this because if they didn't know, they about to know that I am Fauna and I am a boss bitch!

Iceberg outfit fresh to death hoping they don't look too hard at my I.D. I passed thru the long line straight to VIP with my sister's ID that she always let me use. I wasn't old enough to get in a 21 and older club yet but as always I will get my way. As to be expected I get through security and its standing room only. I headed over to VIP where Mr. Chocolate Sensation sat. He stood out from everyone and he was waiting for me. Gawd-Damn! He was looking so good!! I had to secure my expression so it wouldn't be a dead giveaway that I was admiring this dude off rip.

There were other chicks hanging around him and I couldn't hate. They were doing their thang, but it made me wonder, did they get cashed out for a new fit too? I giggled to myself at the thought. It didn't matter because not only was I the baddest bitch in the building, I was the freshest, sexiest and nonchalant bitch in the club that night. That was one thing I didn't do when I was on the job. Yes, locking a paid ass nigga down is considered a job, just to be clear. I didn't believe in getting drunk and acting unladylike. I was on a mission. I walked over to Will and was introduced to Dom-P, and then bottles after bottles were coming back to back! Money was thrown in all different directions that night and ya' girl was treated like a queen!

From that night on, me and Will were together. Even though I had been on trips and other fancy outings with men from my past, it was different with him. Things were happening so fast with this cat, I couldn't keep up with some of the shit he was doing in between. That alone would have been a dead give-away to exposing his hoeish ass ways! The ways that Mrs. King told me about.

Blinded by the bling, overcome by his presence and mesmerized by his manners I was hooked. I think he was too, because he paid for my first apartment and fully furnished it. What added to the beauty of it was what was behind door number seven! Did this nigga cash me out a brand-spanking-new Cadillac DTS to match his?! YES HE DID! He satisfied the fire that burned in me from birth. I wanted more, I was destined for greatness and he treated me as such. I had officially gotten the job. It was then that I started to fall somewhere deep with this man, emotionally.

Through it all I couldn't ignore Mrs. King's voice in the back of my mind saying,

"Fauna are you ready to live a lie?" I tried to block it out, but eventually every time he added something nice to

my neck or wrist, her voice seemed to fade further and further away.

I thought I was in love with this man, and honestly, I thought he was the only man I loved during this time in my life. Not to mention, he wasn't married! I was living it up fa'real and I was finally happy! At least until I found out this nigga was cheating, and then all hell broke loose! He woke me up from my dream... This was not part of the plan. I thought we were in love. Real men don't cheat when they are in love, my Dad didn't and that's all I knew. Fuck the finer things trust is everything so shit had gotten real!

7

"Side Bitch"

Side bitches are the chicken noodle soup for the dope boys' ego. They can have it all at home but still seek the attention of these chicks. Some women purposely look for men that are already in a relationship or married, to avoid the responsibilities that come with it. They just dip in and dip out getting in where they fit in. Benefiting strictly off the good dick and a couple dollars for pocket money. Never much more than that, but I can honestly say, I don't know a bitch out here who hasn't been a side bitch at least once in their lifetime. Knowingly or unknowingly, we all wore those shoes. Now the shoe was on the other foot. I guess this bitch Karma decided to show up. Raggedy hoe!

Nevertheless, these are the bitches Mrs. King told me about who she had to ignore and this is the type of situation she told me I would have to overlook. I guess I can answer her questions now. Hell fuck naw I can't handle this type of shit!! I lost my mind momentarily.

"Who the fuck is she?!" I snapped, catching some Lil Kim-looking-ass-bitch in the front seat of his car on my way to the mall!

"Yo! F!" That's what Will called me when he was caught up in some shit!

"Chill wit all that Ma!" He said defensively.

This nigga was 2 seconds from catching my keys upside his big ass head.

I jumped out my shit heading over toward his side of the car.

"You better answer the muthafuckn' question nigga!!! WHO THE FUCK IS THIS BITCH!!!"
I stared with an evil ass eye over at this small frame sitting on my seat! The BITCH was in *my* seat. I was hired for this position and this hoe was here doing my job, this shit ain't about to fly! So many violent images crossed my mind as my heart began to break even more. Surprised he hadn't pulled off yet, I kneeled down inside his window contemplating on what my next move was gon' be. My feelings were hurt, and Will knew I was a silly and half crazy bitch that would have came out of my stilettos on his ass in a heartbeat! Then this little Chimpanzee had the audacity to speak up! The nerve of this nothing ass side bitch.

"Will, is everything okay?" she asked
This bitch had no idea how she just pushed my button by the sound of her raggedy ass voice.

He had this look on his face that read ... "Bitch, are you nuts! Do you know who the fuck this is?!" He appeared to be really afraid for himself and her at that point. That bitch knew the only time she was allowed to open her mouth was when his dick was going in it! I was ready to murk both of them! Her Lipstick was smeared all on her mouth and his top button of his shorts was unbuttoned. I was ready for some gangsta shit!

I said, "Listen you little BITCH... You need to speak when the fuck spoken to..." I leaned in the drivers' side window pointing my finger in her face.

"F! Chill!"

He couldn't do anything but put his head down.

My eyes got wide as I zoomed in on him and her. The hairs on my neck rose up and I went into a hot flash so intense I damn near set myself on fire!

"F, I'm in the middle of some business. This is my homeboy's girl, F! Come on na!" he tried to explain stumbling over his words

I looked down at his dick that was still semi-hard and then up at her who had this devious grin on her face I wanted to put a bullet through that bitch head at that point.

"Your homeboy who Will?? Her mouth? And as far as this so-called doing business tip you on, where is the business? I don't see shit out in the open Nigga! I ain't five-o! So where is the *business* you claimin?"

I looked around trying to see if something was out in the open I could identify as business, and I be damn!, what I found in the backseat on the floor… This bitch nasty ass G-String! I reached inside and opened the door to the backseat and carefully picked them up with the tips of my nails and said,

"Oh, so how much is this worth muthafucka?!" and threw the G string in his face.

"Maaannnn…" Will said dropping his head in shame.

That was about all he could do before I blacked out on his ass! All I remember is my fist dotting his eye! I don't know what happened to the bitch I guess she knew to get the fuck on. She got ghost in the midst of our chaos! Bitch must of been a track star or something!

I knew when I pulled up on his ass and saw the bitch in his whip it wasn't about no fuckin business! They say Karma's a bitch. Hell, maybe it is, but fuck all that reap what you sow shit. I knew fucking with married men would catch up to me one day, but unlike them weak ass bitches who settled for the bullshit, I have to have a lot invested into the relationship to play the part. If it don't make dollars, it don't make sense to me, flat-the-fuck-out!

I can't lie; I was enjoying every bit of this man until these big booty bitches wanted a piece of my investment. See, I'm a stingy bitch, so sharing wasn't an option for me. Not to mention, the chick I caught him with, wasn't the first and damn sho' wasn't his last! I kept finding out about his cheating ways, but I held on. I thought of the conversation with Mrs. King again & I guess this was the bad I accepted. When I was happy it was all good. But when it was bad, it was fucked up and my heart was tired of being hurt!

Some would call me a fool in love. I accept that. But on a serious note, it wasn't like I wasn't benefiting from it. We had a great relationship in terms of friends, though he lacked respect for what we shared intimately. I was too far gone and had so much invested into this that new or old bitches couldn't turn my attention away from my Will. I knew them other bitches didn't have shit on me any damn way. They may have the beauty and the booty but they damn sure didn't have the brains. I was one of a kind in these streets and Will knew that. He would fuck up but NEVER let me get too far away without reeling me back in. Problem with me was I was following my heart instead of my brain. That wouldn't last for long though.

Looking back on all the bullshit I went through with him after dating that first year, him catching a case and getting 2 years was the ultimate test on our relationship.

Love played a major role in keeping my ass around during his bid and it was almost like a funeral when he left. Although he was alive he was absent from me physically. Not to mention the drama that comes with it. You know how when someone dies, all their secrets hit the fan? It was just more bitches and more problems that surfaced when he left. I had to stay focused though.

Still young and beautiful, I still kept my job at Ford Motor Credit, even though it was nothing like that fast money life I was used to. I was bored as hell but I had to do what the fuck I had to do to make ends meet. I couldn't afford all those trips and nice clothes I was accustomed to but the struggle kept me on my toes when it came to focusing on a new plan to get money. That fire was rekindled, and the Ford Motor Credit checks were certainly no cure. I was taught by my parents to always be appreciative of the opportunities in life no matter what they are. The most mediocre move can be the first step to unlock my potential. I came to terms to living average but I was not sure how long this understanding would last. So for now, having what many considered a bomb ass job with benefits with no college degree was cool.

8

"Who is T-Stuckey?"

The city of Detroit is known for being the automobile capital of the world; The Motor City! Detroit is also famous for its distinctive Motown music sound from the 1960s. The city skyline is beautiful as I cross over Grand River and the Blvd. I can recall taking field trips to Hitsville USA, the home of Motown. So many things run through my mind as I float through these streets. My mind began to reflect of the different changes I've seen in this city in my lifetime. It's a place of people and places, trends and events, world-changing inventions and groundbreaking music. It is also known for organized crime. Detroit, aka "The D" is very well known for drugs and violence. Some make the news, some don't. Everybody claims they are a "D" boy, but in reality REAL "D" boys come far and few in between. See, there are levels to this shit, qualifications to be considered a certified "D" Boy. One required qualification is loyalty. Something this new generation lacks. All you hear on the news and in the streets is how some young dumb full of cum ass little boy has done something stupid and for no reason. These new lil niggas violate all the damn codes. It's a damn shame. It is rare as fuck to meet someone loyal to the streets and also loyal to you. It is a hard task to manage but I was lucky enough to meet a man that mastered it. Someone I still call my good friend to this day, T-Stuckey. I come to the red light at the Boulevard and Lodge and find myself smirking at the way we ran circles around these half ass street niggas and females out here. Our relationship was like no other. He taught me a lot about the legal and illegal sides of making money out here. Our bond was tight and I was able to learn as much as I did because we never stepped outside of handling business and being in the friend zone. I realized any business friendships that didn't involve sex turned out to be the most profitable. It was no secret that all the niggas in the city wanted a taste of me, and all the chicks in the city wanted a taste of him. The thing is, we were untouchable, our pockets were deep and our friendship was a mystery. They swore up and down we were fuckin. We would just laugh at they ass and people hated that shit! When we stepped on the scene we weren't turning heads we was breakin fuckin necks! We had some good ass times back then...Thinking back on how it all started with the man known as T-Stuckey.

As I looked in the mirror my hair was tight and my Chanel shorts were even tighter. There was no question I was gonna turn heads today, like any other day. I had on my platinum Cartier's with the red lens to match the spaghetti strap on my Chanel shirt. I knew I was flyer than an airplane. Now y'all know my feet had to be fresh with my open toe Chanel sandals. That was a must. I'm 20 years old going on 30 is what T would jokingly say. People always tell me I have been here before. At the time my birthday is coming up and I was reaching a milestone, age 21 on the 18th of March. My days of using my sisters I.D. are over. Yes, I can hit the door without holding my breath.

I can hit all the clubs with ease now because one thing for sure, me and my girls always gets it in! Summers in Detroit are the best. I guess we suffer through the winter blast and horrible weather, so Mother Nature treats us to some of the best summers and it was finally here. I was ready looking for some good action.

"Robin hurry up girl we gotta go. Damn you slow as hell!" I hollered across the room.

She yelled back, "A'ight bitch I'm coming. That damn picnic ain't going anywhere. It's only down the street anyway. Damn quit acting thirsty."

"Thirsty?" I looked at her sideways with my hand on my hip. "See that's what I am talking about. Hoes be getting beside they self. You give a bitch an inch she take a foot, bitch hurry yo ass up", I said hoping Robin would move a little faster. "You know I gotta stop by the DRO spot to get me a couple sacks of that good good shit that have a muthafucka gone," I added.

"The DRO spot?! I know you ain't talking about Skinny Mikes spot over off 7 and Evergreen." Robin asked.

"Yes I am and you need to put a pep in yo' step cause dude said he only got a couple sacks left and I need them, all of them," I said looking into my pocket mirror smacking my lips together making sure my lip-gloss was on just right.

"Girl why don't you just roll up some of that Reggie you be selling for Ole boy and save your money?"

"Girl listen I don't get my lungs dirty with that Bama ass weed. If I'm going to blow I will need some fire. Now come on before his ass sells them and for the record I don't sell shit for no nigga. I'm a self-made bitch so don't ever get that twisted." I said grabbing my purse and keys. "I'll be in the car," I said as I closed the door.

I walked outside, the air hit my skin and I felt fresh as ever. My car had to be feeling the same way because it definitely was looking like it. Robin was a few steps behind me.

"Damn Fauna you got the D.T.S. looking like new money. When did you get the car washed?" Robin asked looking surprised.

"Oh, I called them niggaz over on Joy Rd. You know they got that mobile car wash that will come where ever you at and wash your whip," I explained.

"Oh yeah, well you better be careful letting them niggaz know where you lay yo' head. These niggaz is too grimy out here for me," Robin said in a serious tone.

I thought about it momentarily then replied,

"I know but they cool. They're some of Will's people. You know he ain't no lame out here. So if one of them niggaz was to try me like that he would handle it."

Understanding the reality of situation, Robin replied

"Aight girl, I'm just saying. Be cautious about these things now a day."

We pulled off and all I could think about was how crazy this picnic was about to be. First things first, the DRO.

When we got to Skinny Mike's spot as always his ass was trying to holla. The look in his eyes always told the same tale every time I seen him. But who could blame him?

"What's up Robin? What up doe Fauna?" He said smiling like a kid in a candy factory.

"Hey Mike what's up?" We said in unison as if we wanted to hurry up and get straight to the point.

I asked,

"Can I buy a few of those $100 sacks?"

"You know I got you baby girl, but damn can a nigga get some love," he said jokingly but in his mind he was super serious.

Mike ass never ceases to amaze me always trying to steal a feel. He was always trying to work me; not knowing I was a gangsta bitch to the core, me and Robin always worked him. You know how it goes.

You gotta pay to play.

As I gave Mike his usual hug cause he wouldn't serve me if I didn't. He went to try and grab my ass and when he did I slipped those sacks of DRO right out of his hand and Robin grabbed what she could out of the bag he always kept behind the bar. After going through the dramatics of pushing his hands off my ass our job was done. When we got into the car and pulled off we counted 7 sacks of that good good. Damn a free $700 just for a hug. It was worth it every dime!

When we finally pulled up to River Rouge Park it was jam packed, bumper to bumper, rim to rim. There were Benzes, Corvettes, Cadillac trucks and more parked everywhere. You could definitely see why we were called the Motor City.It took us almost 30 minutes to park and get to where the "happenings" were at. When me and Robin stepped out of my DTS it's like everything and everyone stopped. Words could not describe how guys were looking at us. Their bottom lip was on the grass. I have to say the feeling was too good. Young, fresh, and clean!

With the pink Iceberg outfit and pink gator sandals on, Robin had all kinds of dudes on her line. The sun did her long straight hair so much justice. It just glistened at her every move. Stealing the show was an understatement. We *were* the show. As we were walking I noticed a couple guys grouped up talking to this girl I knew. I grabbed Robin's arm and whispered,

"Who is that caramel guy over there looking brand new? I ain't never seen him before."

"Girl your guess is good as mines. But I know that chick standing next to him is that girl Renita who be writing books. Do you want me to go ask her for you?" Robin replied.

"Naw girl! I don't want it to seem like I'm thirsty or something, well it doesn't matter anyway, here she comes," we quickly changed the subject.

"Hey Robin girl. Hey Fauna. Y'all two are looking cute. Fauna girl I like those sandals," Renita said as she admired my attire.

"Thanks girl!" I said smiling and looking down at the bad ass shoes I was wearing.

"So Renita have you been writing any new books? Because my girl Fauna just started reading those urban books and I was just telling her how you be writing them too."

"I'm glad you asked because the bitch at *Triple Crown Publications* just dropped me. But God is too good. My good friend T-Stuckey who just came home said he got my back on whatever I want to do. It's funny because we were just talking about it over there. So you might be seeing me start my own publication company real soon," she said excitedly.

Robin and I locked eyes with one another reading each other's minds. There was no second guessing who the caramel dude was that caught my attention.

T-Stuckey must have noticed us at that point, because I could barely hear him talking to one of his boys over the music and crowd at the park, he asked "Aye cuz look! He said pointing our way "Who are those girls over there talking to Renita?"

I heard his boy Den Den respond, "Aww that's Robin and Fauna. Them hoes from Oak Park and you know Fauna be selling that fire!"

I could feel T-Stuckey's eyes zone in on me. He said, "Yeah I'm a have to holla…."

"Yo cuz, do you see that nigga over there in the green?" Den Den said cutting T-Stuckey off.

"Yeah I see him", T-Stuckey said.

"Well that's the hoe ass nigga who shot me back in the day." Den Den explained.

I stood from afar and could barely make out what they were saying, but I heard enough to know some shit was about to go down. I heard Den Den tell some chicks to bounce because it was about to get real ugly.

Just then I heard T-Stuckey shout out,

"Yo Den Den go get Marv Dog and tell him we need to bounce ASAP!"

"Aight but keep yo eyes open cuz cause that nigga think he slick trying to creep over here all slow and shit." Den Den responded.

T-Stuckey kept his eyes on the prize and said "Yeah I see his ass. One thing fo sho if he knew better he'd do better."

Those were the last words I remember T-Stuckey saying before the shit hit the fan! Marv came roaring across the grass in a '02 green Cadillac Escalade. Den Den jumped in the front seat and T- Stuckey got in the back.

"Damn Robin you see that nigga?" I asked.

"Yeah, I saw his ass trying to creep up on Den Den and them with that gun in his hand. Good thing they jumped in that truck in time. I wanted to yell and tell' em, but they were too far away. I'm glad whoever was driving pulled off before that scandalous ass nigga got too close to them." It's some scandalous ass niggas in the D.

Shots rang out into the air and everyone started running in every direction almost knocking each other down. The next time I looked up I saw the green Cadillac truck going towards Warren but it came to a stop. Then I saw T-Stuckey hop out the backseat and into the driver seat and whoever was driving got into the back. I didn't know what the hell was going on, and then the truck did a 360 and was headed back towards me! It was like a scene from a movie. The way T-Stuckey bobbed and weaved through traffic it looked like a scene straight out the movie Transporter. All I was thinking was why in the hell is he heading back in the direction of the guy who was just shooting. I ran and wondered why am I worried about it and got the fuck on. He finally passed me and what I saw told it all. It was about to go down for real! T-Stuckey stopped the truck right by Big Bob and Mooka who was standing up inside of his drop top Corvette holding a nickel plated A-K 47. All of this shit was unreal; it was so much going on. As the scene unfolded everyone scattered. They spoke for a hot second and in no time all you heard were tires screeching. Everyone was driving back to back headed

51

towards Joy Road. It looked like a car show for people who didn't know what really was going on. All I could think about was somebody might die tonight.

It was weeks before I saw T-Stuckey again. My mind was in shambles as I thought about the action filled picnic. One day B-Man, a friend of Robin's called and asked her if we wanted to go to breakfast.

As she asked me holding the phone I had to let her know,

"Hell yeah girl you know I ain't missing no meals, " I said loud enough for both of them to hear me.

Robin laughed her ass off. B-Man took us to Sweden House over on 12 mile. After we finished eating B-Man said he had someone that he really wanted me to meet and there was no way I could lose in this type of situation because it was always a win win for me. Plus B-Man had that money so if he wanted me to meet someone I knew they had to have that bread too. He already knew what my requirements were.

When we pulled up to the gas station on Evergreen and 696 the bass from the black Escalade sitting on 20's had my complete attention. As we got closer and came just feet away from the guy pumping gas into his truck I could see his every move. When he hung the pump up I watched him go inside his truck and into his glove compartment and grab something and start to wipe his hand. What in the hell was that, a napkin or something I wondered? Nevertheless, I always appreciated good hygiene and nice teeth. The lyrics of Ja Rule's new joint featuring Case roared from the truck. As I stared at him it's like he knew I was looking at him. He looked in my direction and started walking toward the car. Being behind tinted windows it felt like they were clear as the blue sky the way he looked on as he continued to walk towards my direction. He approached the car opened the door and sat right next to me without even acknowledging anyone in the car. I was at a loss for words.

"Yo what up B-man?" He said but looking in to my eyes.

"You man what up doe gangsta?" B-man replied, then looking at me.

"Look I want to introduce you to my friends. Robin this Gangsta and Gangsta this..."

Before B-Man could get the words out they were already being said.

"Fauna, right?" I just nodded.

I was shocked that he knew who I was.

"And you are?" I said for my own personal joy.

"You can call me Terry. But my dudes call me 'T' or 'T-Stuckey'."

Suddenly my mind rewinded to the picnic, I remembered seeing him at River Rouge Park that day but I still had no idea who he was. All I know is the way he moved was electrifying. He moved with grace, power, and complete authority. He was definitely someone I wanted to get to know, I knew I could learn something from him. Before we left T-Stuckey asked me for my number and of course he got it.

The weeks turned into months and every day with T-Stuckey was truly incredible. As time passed I learned that he kept baby wipes in the glove compartment of all his cars. He loved to buy me nice gifts and just spend quality time with me. His aura was to die for. You know how it feels to always want to be around someone? Well that's how we were. Not to mention everyday with him felt like a holiday. Terry gave me so much game about the streets once he found out I was playing in them. Hiding anything from him was something I just didn't do. If he didn't know I told him to make sure he knew it came from me first. That's what kind of effect he had on me. One day I was sitting at home and my phone rang. It was T-Stuckey. I will never forget that day. He asked me if I wanted to go to Franklin's restaurant and have lunch with him. I said yes almost immediately. But the words that came next were completely surprising.

"Well come outside then." He said.

I was cheesing hard as hell but stayed calm. I was happy as hell but I stayed on top of my game not missing a step. I went outside and the sight before me was to die for. The blue drop top Corvette with the blue top sitting on them chrome choppers made my panties wet. Once I was inside the smell of fresh leather was everywhere. As we ate lunch and finished Terry invited me back to his condo on Jefferson Avenue.

When we walked inside my breath was taken away. He had flat screens everywhere, the first flat screens I had ever seen to be exact. The kitchen was designed completely in stainless steel and his entire place was plushed out. That shit looked like something out of "The Robb Report" and none of that "Art Van" furniture store shit. The smell of the condo was so fresh but what I seen next was the sexiest shit I seen in Detroit so far. The view of Canada and downtown was astonishing literally. I wasn't even entertaining the idea of leaving there anytime soon. Terry had left and went to his bedroom leaving me to make myself at home. When he returned he had a bag in his hand. He gave it to me and I reached inside and pulled out a box. It was a pair of red Ferragamo shoes inside. I looked into his eyes and I know he saw a little too much happiness. But I had to let him know how I was feeling.

"Terry I hope you don't think I'm giving you some pussy just because you bought me an expensive pair of shoes." I explained.

"Hold up baby girl. First and foremost if you did offer me some pussy just because I bought you these shoes I definitely wouldn't fuck you. If that's all it takes to get it I really would be cool on you. Baby girl I ain't gone lie, I'm feeling you and I definitely want to get to know you for real. I am normally a pretty good judge of character and you haven't proven me wrong yet. But on another note I hope you enjoy the gift a'ight?" He said walking towards the kitchen and looking in the fridge.

"Thank you so much Baby." I said smiling.

This man was unbelievable. One of the many qualities I loved about Terry was it was always a lesson and blessing while being around him. I eventually told Terry about Will and how dudes were playing him now that he was locked up. He said he heard of him but didn't know him. Terry told me if I was serious about him now was the best time to get to know him and hold him down. When a person goes to jail there true colors and feelings come into play. He told me if I did what a real woman would do for someone she cared for, that person would give them the world or die trying.

Time was flying and that coming Christmas I received one of the greatest gifts ever. With a little help from my sister, he wanted to do something extra special so she suggested getting me something that will always remind me of him. Terry bought me a dog. In fact I still have that dog to this day. "Papi" is his name and Terry is his daddy. Every day I see my dog it reminds me of Terry, so his little plan worked.

As Christmas came and went my B-day was quickly approaching and I wanted to do it big. I had really been doing well for myself. You know the saying "you work hard then you play even harder." With the help and guidance of T-Stuckey and a few others I was finally getting myself into the position that I wanted to be in. Terry's B-day was also coming up. His was on the 21st of March and mine was on the 18th. He knew this of course, and him being how he is, he felt I deserved nothing but the best. To make matters even better he wanted to celebrate our B-days together. How could I resist? With me and him together we were gonna shut Detroit down and definitely make it a night to remember. A Babe and a Ballers Birthday Bash was one of my first big parties. The summer of 2001 was another lesson and blessing for me.

Terry was always about his money and he made a lot of it. He launched a clothing line called "Personal Appearance." He specialized in T-shirts and hats. I admired him so much being that he had just come home from prison and was so goal driven. With the amount of determination he possessed he made everything he set forth into a reality. That was true power and I must say it was so sexy. What took me was that I watched the hip-hop Mayor of the country *Kwame Kilpatrick* from Detroit wear and even promote some of Terry's T-shirts, specifically the "C.E.O." line. *Kwame* even wore his clothing line the day of his election becoming the youngest mayor in the world. He also wore Terry's T-shirts when he worked out. He had several slick sayings on his shirts that the hood was going crazy for. From the "stop snitching" shirts, to the "D.B.A." (Detroit Ballers Association), and many more.

I was so impressed with his work ethic. He became a semi idol to me. As far as getting this paper, I must say his ambition and ideas even rubbed off on me. That's why today I own a successful clothing line specializing in t-shirts and designs. As Terry continued to pursue many businesses ventures I knew this was just the tip of the iceberg. Terry called me one day to meet him at Chucks Millionaires Club to holla at a couple of his guys pertaining to promoting our party. I remember when I pulled up to Chucks Millionaires Club on Plymouth Road I was a little anxious. See I believed in Terry but you know how the saying goes "Don't believe it until you see it", but I must say he showed me.

Never again did I second guess a thing he said or said he was gonna do.

Terry introduced me to his friends Mike Lee and Terry Arnold. Terry Arnold was the program director for the second biggest radio station in Detroit 105.9 and his family owned it. But FM98 WJLB was the hottest radio station in the city so to be talking to the people of the 2nd hottest I was ecstatic. Terry had connects for real. I remember him telling me how he met Rubin Rodriguez who owned Red Ink Records, who also had Busta Rhymes signed to their label, and how he was trying to help him promote his record label and his artists. I was just thankful and grateful to be in his presence. When Terry said he was gonna do something or make it happen that's exactly what he did.

The determination and thoughtfulness and his care for the ones he loved was indescribable. I just loved how he always wanted me to be part of what he was doing. He even let me sing the hook on one of his songs on his album and I can admit I am not that great at singing he just believed in me like that. Terry truly cared and had love for me and really wanted to see me prosper in life.

My birthday couldn't come fast enough. With all the promotion and effort me and T-Stuckey put into it I knew this day was gonna be one to remember by many. Terry wanted me to receive the recognition that I deserved. He knew the qualities I possessed and the loyalty I could give so he knew he had to go all out and that's just what he and I did. When that party came being recognized was an understatement. Terry was looking so handsome. The thoughts I had in my mind were ones to keep to myself. I nonetheless was definitely shutting it down. The customized designer dress by Gi Gi Hunter which was my favorite color red hugged my hour glass frame like honey on my skin. I also had on at least $75,000 thousand worth of jewelry.

I was the poster child for the saying, "diamonds are a girl's best friend."

Without further ado T-Stuckey had on two tone pair lavender gators with the matching belt. Lavender pants and blazer by Lou Miles. The rose gold Rolex he had on had too many admirers. He actually was the first one in the city with one. He wore almost $300 thousand worth of jewelry himself. That night the party was phenomenal. There were ice sculptures with my name and T-Stuckey's name. It was so many seafood dishes it was crazy. Chocolate covered strawberries. Plenty of champagne and cognac.

We had a V.I.P. section too. If you bought that 100 dollar ticket you had access to the V.I.P ROOM with free drinks all night. I was called to the stage by surprise. Terry had the group "4 Men" perform for me and serenade me on stage. Terry also performed songs from his latest album "72 Hours". Along with a performance by him, E-Dubb, Big Dogg, Monte Ski from DMW (Detroit's Most Wanted), Five Ella, and "the Puritan Army", they shut that stage down. There were at least 1,500 tickets sold. The police even started to turn guests away by blocking off the street that led to the front door of the International Market Place in downtown Detroit where the party was held. That night Detroit recognized me forever and in more than one way. As Terry and I walked around our entourages were also to be reckoned with. Terry had all of his guys laced in nothing but suits and gators straight from Walter at "The Broadway and Tommy from "City Slickers". Terry was extremely likeable. He wanted everyone to shine who deserved it. That night he made sure the best of the best was in my presence. I'll never forget it.

One day I was riding along with a friend down in ATL on Peachtree Road in my brand new big yellow ass hummer. I couldn't believe my eyes when a brand new CL 500 AMG Mercedes Benz sitting on some fly ass 20 inch Lowenharts rode right pass me. I thought to myself about the saying "everyone has a twin" but not today. I know my eyes weren't deceiving me especially after seeing those Michigan plates! So I two-wayed Terry and asked him where he was. He hit me right back asking where I was. I hit him back and told him I was in Atlanta looking at him in his brand new birthday present. He didn't believe me but when I described that beautiful car and what he had on he knew it was true.

About an hour later me and my guy friend I knew from ATL were inside Gladys Knight's chicken and waffles when my two-way went off again. Shocked it was Terry asking me where I was. I hit him back and asked him where he was. He said Gladys Knight's chicken and waffles looking at me. He then told me to meet him by the bathroom. As I got to the bathroom the sight before me was even better than earlier. I hugged him and he squeezed me tight. Something was wrong, I could feel it. Time flew past and by the time I got back to the table with my friend I noticed his facial expression. He wasn't too happy. We ate then left saying very few words to one another. I didn't care because the way I was feeling only God knew.

September 2001 was one of the worst months around the country because of 9-11. But September in 2002 changed my life forever. A man I deeply cared for was stripped from my presence and his freedom. The pain I began to feel for him and myself was indescribable. I kept hearing all the bogus charges streaming from drugs, murder, money laundering, and witness tampering. These charges set forth in him being punished beyond my wildest dreams. They issued an order to seek the death penalty against someone I cared so much about. I couldn't fathom the thought of them trying to kill Terry. If I had anything to do with it they weren't. Yeah, over my dead body.

As time elapsed and his trial came and went, I was devastated by the bad news of him being found guilty and sentenced to life in prison. I learned how the government lied on him so bad just because they had it in for him, a Black successful young man. One thing I do know is Terry was a fighter. I learned that he fought extremely hard against the United States of America, mainly an over jealous prosecutor. I heard his good friend E-Dubb testified on his behalf. His good brother Dwight Smith that played for Tampa Bay who won the Super Bowl in '03 also testified on his behalf. But as you all know who have loved ones in prison the government doesn't play fair. Terry's grandfather M.C. was also indicted by the FEDS. They had no remorse for no one. He later died before trial. I was unable to communicate with Terry during the trial due to the max custody they had him in. I wanted to comfort him and provide him with the love and help he deserved. As the years passed so did visits and phone calls. So much has happened since Terry has been incarcerated it's sad thinking about it. The good niggas leave us one way or the other while these bum as nothing ass niggas continue to live without a purpose. Terry is a wonderful man but the pain was just beginning. He lost his grandfather and then his cousin "Proof" from the hip hop group "D-12" with Eminem. He was in so much pain I just wished I could have held him just for just one minute. One thing for sure God is great and if you're reading this Terry I'll see you soon & if the Lord is willing it will be on the streets and not in that hell hole.

9

"Money Power Respect"

It was New Years Eve, 2000, and I just came from buying a bunch of canned goods and water after hearing some crazy 'end-of-the-world' rumor that was supposed to happen on New Years. I usually don't fall victim to the hype but this shit was like a national situation so I'd rather be safe than sorry. I may be on the smaller side but a bitch loves to eat good. I had all the supplies that flashed across the screen but now I was ready to hit the streets, potential natural disaster and all! It was time to party with my girl Robin. This bitch knew how to get it in! I was always so laid back and boring. After Will went in the birdcage, I pretty much just worked and went to bed afterwards. It was like I lost that drive to reach that next level in my life. He was gone and took my drive with him. It was like my life was stuck in traffic and I didn't have gas nor brakes. Many would call my situation in the hustle game someone on the verge of giving up but deep inside I knew it was my heart longing for my man. Meanwhile my mind was like fuck feelings bitch and create a master plan.

Me and Robin had become roommates after Will went to jail and, she experienced firsthand, my boring-ass-life. This night in particular I just knew it was going to be a night to remember. We got FRESH TO DEATH and hit the bricks! I was slowly getting my groove back. I remember it like yesterday. The club lights flashed across the dark room. I was out in the middle of the dance floor with my crazy ass BFF doing some dance that obviously caught the eye of another victim, oops, I mean volunteer! I saw him looking so I kept on grooving. I knew of him and the little that I did know was enough to make him qualify for some of my time. "O" was what the streets called him. Once we locked eyes, I started putting on a sexy ass performance like the bitch in New Jack City! Hair swinging, ass popping, he couldn't resist. Within moments of stealing every bitch shine in that room, I had the wealthiest dude in the building! The vision I had of him at first glance sent me into a gold-digging battle zone. I saw dollars that made a lot of damn sense! And like usual I was determined to get what I wanted. I was standing at the bar rocking an expensive ass Coogi outfit topped off with the Franck Muller watch and plenty VVS Diamonds, a bitch was worth every diamond I was rocking that night! Next thing I knew, he had one of his groupies approach me requesting that I meet up with him at a table he had in the VIP section. I took him up on his offer, swaying my hips in his direction. Within moments of exchanging names and drinks, we shared some small talk. It was not long after that when I found myself very impressed with this man. He was saying all the right shit to get it that night, which is a behavior I don't usually practice when meeting a guy! But, that nigga O coulda' got it! In other words, I would have broken all the rules with good reason.

Things moved really fast after that night! This man not only looked out for me, like most men I dated, but this was a learning experience for me. He taught me the ins and outs of the game, which I was oblivious too. I grew more attracted to his mind. I knew dude had countless women, but I wasn't trippn' on that shit. Get in where I fit in, was my motto. It's hard out here for a Pimpstress! Armed with enough information to move forward on dude, I invited him over the next day. The way our apartment was set up, we had a huge picture window where we could see who pulled up to our spot. When I say dude looked like a million bucks pulling into the lot, I mean, I felt like I had hit the jackpot. In my mind I was already picking out my next whip, outfit, hairstyle, and I was spending dude's money and *he ain't even know it.* He was walking right into my trap!

We went to *Morton's,* and had a whole room to ourselves. I could tell this man was well respected, and his demeanor was that of a boss! Maybe it was his demeanor that grabbed my attention that night. I am just glad we connected because he was showing me things that no man had. He spoke about having to leave town on business the next day, and asked me would I take him to the airport. I said yes, of course. I liked what I saw and wanted to learn more about this 'O' dude. His walk intrigued me, his conversation inspired me and the way he made moves soothed my mind. I was the student again and I LOVED it. The date with him moved so fast that, before I knew it, he had dropped me off, with no sex. He didn't even throw hints. He was different and I loved it. He told me how much he enjoyed my company. I learned later that he dated beautiful women, but none as spunky and smart like myself. Although school was never my priority your girl is far from dumb. Total package certified book Smart street smarts. Just more weapons in my arsenal.

Being that I couldn't read minds, and he was short with how this 'taking him to the airport plan' was supposed to play out. He told me he would stop by to pick me up first thing in the morning, and I just figured we would take my car. To my surprise, dude pulled up in a new Benz with some dope ass rims and all kind of features on it to drop him off in. I only knew this dude for less than 24 hours and he was leaving me with his new whip!

*'I wish he didn't trust me so much...*from the *Bobby Womack* song played in my head. My parents played old school music and danced in the living room almost every Friday night. I was too young to understand the sacrifices they made. Hell what about the sacrifice O just made knowing this car is worth more than anything I owned at this point. Like a Boss he tossed me the keys to drive him to his destination, gave me a small peck on the lips, and I waited to hear from him on what to do next. What I thought would be immediate instructions on where to drop off his car, turned out being just the opposite. I ended up keeping it for over 4 months! Welcome to the good life. I was happy as hell.

From that day forward we would talk damn near all day and night about some of *everything*. I guess I had *'Niggaz Can Trust A Bitch'* written on my forehead. I mean for him to just leave me his expensive ass new car in exchange for no pussy, no head, and very little conversation, this shit was crazy. It wasn't long before I was on a flight to AZ a couple times to bring him some money he had me pick up for him. I never asked questions, I know the rules. I'd just fulfill the duties of my job and look beautiful in between time. More importantly he started giving me my cut, at least ten racks every time I came. A bitch was sitting pretty each time too! But, what stood out in the back of my mind more than anything? Was the fact that he hadn't tried to get the pussy at all at that point. I had access to more than most and he never ever tried it. It totally had me baffled but for the love of money and luxury who gives a damn about fuckin or suckin. I was getting money. It wasn't until later when I found out he had bigger plans for me.

I learned over time O wasn't the mixing-business-with-pleasure type of dude. I was forced to accept that through a few cold showers and some self-inflicted orgasms. I ain't gon' lie... I was like one of those niggas that get with a chick and have those high expectations, thinking at any given moment they're going to get the pussy real quick and don't! Just being around O, I could tell the dick was lovely based on his demeanor. But, I respected his position, and after getting money with dude, I accepted his position and placed the idea of ever having some hot-butt-naked sex with him on the back-burner. Like Eric B and Rakim said in their *'I Ain't No Joke'* hit... *I Saved It and Put It In My Pocket For Later... '* All and all, O knew I would be more useful to him without all the emotional attachments, and he was right. Shit could get real ugly when you mix dick and pussy together, I swear. I saw it with my own eyes happen plenty times before. So, over time I learned this was his way of making sure shit wouldn't get crazy between us and you know what? - Fauna was okay with that. A bitch was really growing up at this point. I was loyal, which didn't always come his way in friends or family. To sum it all up... I was his four-leaf clover, his lucky charm.

A few months after meeting O I looked up and had about $87,000 saved up from running errands for him. When he was back in town from his AZ trip, he came over to my apartment, and sat back on the couch and rolled up. It was a very relaxed moment... finally. I could tell the "open" sign for the business was "closed" for the time being allowing him to chill. Considering we were no longer "at work", I wondered *'Could this be it?'* My freaky-horny-ass was pondering on the idea of us possibly gettin' it in right then. Business was closed but my legs and mouth was open for business. A bitch started discreetly exercising her jaws and shit preparing to give this nigga the best head of his life! I found myself so relaxed around him at that point I just blurted out something that's been on my mind since the day we locked eyes.

"O, I wanna talk to you about something I've been holding back for a minute..."

"Oh yea?" he said with this grin looking down in his lap making me feel a little uneasy.

I wasn't going to let his little childish grin hold me back from what the fuck I wanted to say!

Hell! I'm a boss bitch and Fauna gets what Fauna wants got-dammit! I said to myself, trying to grow balls the whole time I was sitting next to his sexy ass! The nigga smelled good, looked good and I knew right then the dick was just as good, so here I go....

"I got a lil money saved up and I wanted to send a few chips with you the next time you Re-up. In so many words, I would like to make an investment with you."

Ahhh hah! Yall muthafuckas thought a bitch was gon' let a nigga know what I was really feeling right then! Hustle over horny, remember that. But I ain't gon' lie... the moment was right and I was sure by the expression on his face he knew I was about to crack on some dick-me-down type shit, but I fooled all y'all asses, him too and kept the shit business because that's what boss bitches do. Money Power Respect muthafuckas! He had that look in his eyes that appeared a little confused. I was trying to read his ass which wasn't a skill I had yet conquered. Yet I knew it was definitely a future requirement in this line of work. Getting into this niggas head was damn near as difficult as *Superman* trying to see through kryptonite! But, after what I asked of him processed over a few puffs from the blunt, there was a moment of silence, then his entire behavior changed, and it was like he was watching his daughter take her first steps. He was proud that like him, I wanted more, I was content but yearned for much more. This turned him on in a way that the baddest bitch couldn't. He smirked, nodding his head as he pulled smoke from the blunt and then passed it to me.

I said, "What?", and my eyebrows met one another as I stared at him.

That's when keynotes fell from his tongue and I received his words like one of my favorite hit songs.

"You know baby-girl, me not trying to get the pussy from you all this time, wasn't easy. But it was for good reason. I have mad respect for you in many ways, not only as a woman who gets what she wants out of life, but as a grown ass woman who will stand by her word and will do whatever she has to… do or die! You're a risk taker and a muthafuckn' money maker which I trust and love about you girl."

He sat back against the couch resting one arm over the back of it flowing like lyrics to one of the greatest rappers of all-time hit songs.

"This was a part of my plan with you because…" he smiled as he rubbed his chin and then continued. "I knew we was gon' get rich together, and I didn't need no feelings involved in gettin' this money."

As bad as we both wanted to fulfill each other's sexual needs it was superseded by our burning desire for greater wealth and a better life. I stared in his eyes and not once doubted his intention. I believed in him and most importantly, I believed in us! We were in so deep without ever physically fuckin. He made love to my mind and my bank account proved it. I quickly got over the sexual intentions and got focused on the future.

"LET'S GET THIS MONEY THEN!!!"

I high-fived him, passed him the blunt and we sat back on the couch, and focused on a plan that led to our next money mission together.

10

"My First Mil"

Shortly after the last encounter with O, I started traveling back and forth to AZ every time he went. My job at Ford had damn near ran its course, and they were tired of me calling off. Hell I had money to get to. So I did what most people do when approached with other money-making opportunities. I quit! The hustle money outweighed the legitimate money and it was too fucking good! I had reached a level that I always dreamed of and not with my beauty. I got there with my brains. Being a beautiful bitch does not automatically give you the right to not use your noodle. My beauty may get me in the door but it's my brain and loyalty that always seals the deal. Not only was I introduced to his connect, but he showed me how to run an empire from A to Z, I'm not talk'n small time either! I'm talk'n hundreds of thousands every month! Every move I made came calculated with every experience I educated myself with from fucking with older men.

While other women were falling in love with the dick, I was falling in lust with the game. Fuck those cats out there balling backwards! You want to get next to me, spend with me and that's exactly what they ended up doing! I was young but I knew things way beyond my years. I was a sponge absorbing all the knowledge that was readily available to me. My best teachers were my relationships I had been in; dealing with successful street men all the way to very educated legal men. I had a taste of both worlds and knew how to play the game no matter where you dropped the dice. Don't get me wrong, there was some bullshit that came with these fly-by-nighters, but experiences like these wouldn't be what they are if they didn't share a little drama. By the age of twenty-one I had cut out the middle man and had my own connect. I had a few million dollars in cash staring at me on my nightstand. O was proud of me. The way he winked and smiled over at me with those pearly whites was like a king honoring his queen. Although we were more like business partners than two people with this crazy attraction for another, dude was very experienced at putting the pussy-on-ice thang and I loved that shit. This was a strategic move on his part that made a bitch rich.

"*Ooooooo... bayybee...*" I purred as I stared in my bathroom mirror that was attached to my master bedroom.

I could see the money stacked neatly through my peripheral in the mirror.

I thought to myself,

'*Damn Bitch... You got a million muthafuckin' dollars of your own money! YOU DID IT MA! You fuckin' DID IT!!*'

I had successfully fulfilled that burning sensation that always wanted more, needed more. Well that fire was put to rest as I observed the fruits of what some may consider labor.

It took me a minute to fully understand the importance of the saying,

'*The best secret is within self*'.

The less others knew about anything, the safer I was. Making the kind of bread I was making put me on the most wanted list for all kinds of haters. I was the talk of the streets. Niggas and bitches knew about the stamp I made on the city. Real talk, I was an original 'Female American Gangsta'! I was still traveling back and forth to AZ, hooking up with my Mexican connects, and they absolutely loved ya girl! I was nevah' short wit' mines! Even if the load got hit, I was willing and ready to pay whatever I had to, to keep shit moving.

Just to give you a little visual of the kind of bitch I was, one Christmas in 2001, I bought all my girls and the Mexicans family brand new Rolexes and Mink Coats. Now these muthafuckas could barely speak English, but when I slapped some diamonds on their wrists and expensive furs on their backs, English became more of their first language. *For the love of money,* just as O promised and damn I was getting money! Before I could watch my money grow, things started getting crazy! I wanted to spend so bad, the idea of cashing out a new convertible Lexus for the summer and Hummer for the winter came really easy. From there I upgraded to a nice crib in the burbs for myself and every color iced out Rolex watch with earrings, necklace and bracelet to match each one!

It was DIAMONDS DIAMONDS DIAMONDS EVERYWHERE!!! I made it and without using my pussy either. It was greater and deeper than sex. This was the life people still dream of.

There's a scene straight out of the movie *American Gangster* when Frank Lucas (played by Denzel Washington) wore a Chinchilla just to please his woman at a fight and later gets pointed out of the crowd as one of the key players. He then got bumped up to the top of the FEDS list all because he was too damn flashy! He burned that muthafucka after that, and now I started experiencing the same thing. The more I flossed new shit, the more I was getting what many in the game call, "unnecessary attention" that eventually came with problems. It was uncommon for a young woman my age to be out here getting this kind of money in the streets of Detroit. To my knowledge, there was only a few of us. People started wondering who and what I was doing to look this damn good! I could literally hear the whispers when I would go out to different places.

"She got to be fuckin a ballplayer!"

"I know right!"

"Naw, that bitch wit' dude from the eastside. What's his name? Damn, I can't think of his name, but I heard he was paid as hell!"

I mean these nosy ass bitches had envy written all in their fake ass smiles. Even when they would compliment me on some sweet shit I was rockin, I could clearly tell they wish they were me!

Like my mans *Drake said,*

"A bunch of handshakes from the fakes!"

None of that stopped my swerve though, I stayed focused and put in hours like a day-to-day job on how I was going to turn that 1 mil into 2 and that 2 into 10. I was just that hungry to be one of the richest bitches in the "D" with all eyes on me.

11

"Rumors"

How do rumors get started? They're started by the jealous people, and they get mad about something they had, and somebody else is holding. They tell me temptation is very hard to resist" I sang the "Rumors' lyrics in my head. I remember hearing my parents play their Club Nouveau – Rumors Record on Friday nights. I never paid attention to the realism in the lyrics until I was grown.

Okay, so word in the streets was that O was on a hit list to be robbed. This brought on a lot of stress that him, his family and myself didn't need. Before I could inhale all of that shit I found myself experiencing the same thing. The more I flossed new shit, the more the rumors came my way. Multiple people that circulated in the streets were saying some of the same shit about me! I was on that same list and it was all about watching both my back and my front from that point forward. I had refused to get caught off guard! In Detroit when you hear a nigga say "rob", you pay close attention! VERY close attention because there are more people starving than it is niggas balling. Everybody ain't eating. The D was known for having a bunch of lookin-ass-niggas that ain't got shit, trying to steal the ones that shine by all means necessary. These set-yo-ass-up-in-a-minute muthafuckas ain't to be fucked wit' which forced me to pay close attention. I had to make sure I wouldn't get stung out here in these streets. I was trying not to get caught slipping, so I had to make some drastic changes to my appearance. It was all about thinking smart.

As my thoughts ran wild about all the shit that was going on in my life, I had a list of shit I had to do this particular day. I jumped in my whip and headed up the Southfield freeway on one of those nice Detroit summer days. I turned up one of my old school jams that I had just bought the other day, when my phone rang. It was Will calling collect from the joint. In spite of all the new things going on in my life, we were still in touch. He held a special place in my heart and I could never repay him for all he did ... Or at least that's what I thought. We spoke for a few minutes and I let him know how nothing much had changed but the game. What I had going on in the streets didn't affect the fact that a bitch was still a team player who road with this nigga like Bonnie and Clyde through his entire bid. I love who I love and I am loyal even when I have every right not to be. I learned the loving and forgiving way of life from my Mom. No matter how dirty my hands got I always applied the morals instilled in me. He loved my loyalty; they all did, we had this solid foundation for a lasting friendship even when the love was gone. We continued to chat but I knew he was holding back something. I wasn't sure if his hesitation came from the recorded calls or if the words he held were too bad for him to spit out. I became concerned as he began to read me my rights. He knew everything, what I told him thru prior conversations but he also knew the stuff I kept to myself. The streets were talking and Will was definitely listening. Being behind bars didn't mean shit! It was crazy how he had outside resources to bring him gossip from the streets about ya girl! Some true, some lies, you know how it goes. Don't know whether this was good news or bad for a nigga who life has been put on hold to hear how good a sista was doing out here. The fact still remained that people wanted to know who this nigga was who was buyin' me all this shit! Will was the man up in the joint, so anything and everything he would hear going on in the streets came from multiple sources. He had to filter out which information was informative and accurate and what was rumors and bullshit!

One thing he told me not to do was go back up to *Big Bob Car Wash* on 7mile anymore. He told me those Lil Goons in the hood was talk'n' about robbin me! My heart fluttered with fear because I thought they was like family and I patronized their business faithfully! It didn't stop there with the-Will-rundown. There was more street bullshit! There was an incident at the car wash that he heard about and it was so on point I knew it wasn't bullshit! He knew details down to the clothes I was rock'n to the designer bag I had on my arm (a pink LV purse). I had just got that bitch too! Not to mention, I had seventy racks stuffed in it!! Ignorance is bliss, and I don't know what kind of shit I was on to even expose that kind of money to a bunch of hungry ass Negros! Hell, I felt safe around them fools, so I thought! Never once did I ever think I was in harm's way! But I had to remind myself that money is the root of all evil. If you know how rumors float, they go out one way, and come back another. Before I could inhale some sleeze from this good ass Caribbean weed that had just hit the streets this particular day, me having seventy racks in my purse went up to a hundred racks in my purse and that shit spread like wild fire!

Will had much respect in the streets, which meant a

muthafucka better had thought twice before fucking with me and mines! I was feeling a little relieved that Will had things under control and assured me I had nothing to worry about, but there was still this everyday fear that forced me to stay on top of my own shit in case that one muthafucka grew some balls!! I kept my head on the swivel because you just never know. Then I got word that these two dusty ass Niggas that I clearly remember were the ones all in my shit when I was being being serviced. Frontin' like they were on some admiration shit, well they ended up dead! I was a little relieved when I first heard the news thinking 'two less bitches I had to worry about'. And in the back of my mind I thought,

Did this nigga handle this shit for me?'

Well, they say don't ask questions and you won't be a witness to answer them in front of the wrong muthafuckas one day. So I left well enough alone and kept it movin. I knew my Boo Will would be coming home next month so until then, a bitch was single and having fun until the other half arrived!

Ya' girl was having a muthafuckn' ball! I was going to all the major events from All-Star and Super Bowl games, to fights in Las Vegas, stage plays, hair shows, and concerts (backstage VIP of course). I even stepped my game up and went to a few political events, operas and musicals. I was expanding my horizons because I knew the sky was the limit. Hell political science majors are the biggest illegal getting money ass people anyway so I felt at home amongst they ass. Spending fifty thousand or more every time I took a trip was an adventure for me and everyone in my circle! I loved my girls! We were like sisters we never had, and I wanted them to enjoy the fruits of my labor so I paid for *everything*! We hung with nuthin but the best! Just to name a few, my BMF family, NBA, NFL and entertainers. You name them, I rolled with them. I remember giving the Rapper *Jeezy* five thousand in cash while at the casino this one time. We was hanging out after he had lost all he had on him. Dude loved my gangsta mentality and the way my bling blinded his ass!

Before I knew it, I was starting to demand respect everywhere I went just like I was taught. People loved my sassy but confident personality everywhere! I remember me and my home-girl Robin was in Miami for Memorial Day, and was hanging out with Rapper Beanie Sigel, Freeway and the whole State Property family. We sat around and talked shit as usual. They had a suite with a private swimming pool so Robin and I ran back to our room to grab our radio we took everywhere we traveled. It was a Hello Kitty radio that was the cutest little thing that would surprise you and blow your fuck'n eardrums out. We put on some Jay-Z, making sure to keep the music selection in their family. Beanie Sigel switched the music to this bomb ass beat that played over and over again that stuck in my head. Never would I think their hit song "Roc The Mic" would be written on Hello Kitty! Feeling powerful was an understatement. It was a surreal feeling, and I became overwhelmed. It was then when my life was moving in a direction and a speed I couldn't control. It was like falling down a dark hole not knowing what awaits me at the bottom.

My life was an endless journey but it was the life I yearned for and to my surprise my destiny had more in store.

12

"Daddy's Home"

Daddy was home and it was time to play. Yeah I was living the lifestyle of the rich and famous, but a part of me felt a little unbalanced. I wasn't able to put my finger on it but something was missing from this beautiful puzzle. I was happy Will was home but the unfaithfulness that plagued our relationship before he left began to taunt my mind again now that he's here. I thought about it for a 1/2 second then it was back to living my life. I was having so much fun that Will's return home really wasn't much of an issue for me. Hell, having as many hoes as he had, I was on some other shit while those wanna-be-wifey bitches competed for a ring. I fell so madly in love with the game and how well it was paying off; when he got home I lost interest in having a relationship with him. One thing about O that I highly respected was how he felt loyalty was everything and Will wasn't loyal enough to me at that point!!

My phone rang and I was busy at the time, so I missed the call. In my mind I felt they would call back if it was something important. If not, fuck em was how I felt. I was counting money. I didn't really think anything of the first time my phone rang until whoever it was calling started calling again back to back.

"This shit better be an emergency!" I yelled out irritated by the countless rings in between what I was trying to do.

"Sup doe!" The deep familiar voice said on the other end.

It was Will. Now usually, when I answer the phone when he calls I would get that pre-recorded message from the operator saying it was a collect call bullshit. Not this time. This call sound like it was coming from a car or some shit which had my heart racing!

"Wait, Will?" I released a faint chuckle.

"You sound surprised" he said.

"Uhhh yeah! What's up? You out?" I asked trying not to sound too excited

"Where you at?" He ignored my question and kept asking about my whereabouts.

Will called me soon as he hit the pavement! Though he kind of caught me off guard, this was my nigga. We had history. And me being the loyal bitch I am, I dropped everything I was doing, took a few of the stacks I was counting, threw that shit in a bag and pulled up on him. I would be lying if I said the nigga wasn't looking like my favorite piece of candy right then. Mr. Chocolate Sensation was back and better than ever. It's crazy how you can feel one way until you see a nigga looking his best. Before I knew it old feelings start to arise. The flame was rekindled, no lighter required, it was true love, it felt so real.

We talked about how he was proud of me, and how he would do anything for me. I never doubted Will wouldn't go that extra mile for me. I knew in my heart he would. *'Saks Fifth Avenue can't buy affection,'* was such a true statement, I thought as I sat there listening to him talk all this good shit any woman would want to hear. That nigga came with all his fishing equipment. He had his bait, his fishing hook, and was ready to reel my ass back in right then and there. I was vulnerable too! I was a pretty bitch that had it all except for someone I shared something deep with who in turn would feel the same way. That's it! That's what I was missing. I come from a two parent home; my Father was hands on and always there. He provided and made sure we were secure.

Although I was a grown ass woman my soul yearned for that male presence, the security and most of all some good ass dick that was all mine. Despite having millions in my pocket, he was the balance I lacked & no money could buy that balance I needed. Life was good! I had a couple million of my own money. I could damn near buy anything I wanted but I always had to worry about the goons of Detroit. The D was, and still is a grimy place to live. Though I hate to admit it, what you hear is what it is. The only people who beg to differ are people like me who were born and raised here. It becomes a part of you. So when we hear all the bullshit on the news and look at our death, crime and rape statistics, it really doesn't affect us like it would others who are not from here. You become numb to the senseless violence.

We are the most feared city in the world. Shit was so bad; one couldn't trust their best friend! Even they will set yo' ass up!!! There was so much vindictive shit going on in the streets that I had to make an executive decision. It was at that point in my life where I only sold to big dope dealers. If you made under a certain amount, you couldn't even speak to me! This wasn't out of arrogance or me portraying this stuck up image. This became about my life. And I fuckin loved me! When it came to doing business in the streets with these high rollers, surprisingly, it came easy to me. Women don't earn the same respect as men out here. They look at us as pushovers. So ask me what was different about me than the average bitch getting money in the streets of Detroit? Well I think just like these muthafuckin niggas out here!! They can't see the bitch in you, because if you snooze, you lose. I had to tighten up my attitude, become aggressive in my tone and let these cats know I don't fuck around! They fell right in line, eating out of the palm of my hands, all with a hidden agenda that one day they would get an opportunity to taste my pussy.

That was one of my strong points too! I knew most of them if not all of them wanted to fuck me. This was what kept me on top and I learned the true knowledge that pussy was in fact KING! These hungry ass niggas would do anything if they thought they stood a chance. I had this flirtatious way about me, but I was careful on how far to go with it. That was the strategy behind a bitch getting what she wanted. The make believe and the fantasy. But this game is like chess, when playing it takes a lot of concentration in knowing what one's next move will be. I wasn't a pro, I have to admit, but I studied moves closely and always tried to be one step ahead to avoid getting fucked. Every piece to the puzzle holds a strong position, which can be overlooked if one is not careful in making strategic moves. Daddy was home to reclaim his position in the kingdom that I created. I was ready.

13

"The Goons"

Cruising through the streets of Detroit smoking good and looking even better. Wind blowing in my hair, Cartier's grace my face. I'm a D girl fa sho! Money on my mind as usual. I swear I been here before, but had to be as a nigga. The way my mind was set up I know for sure I wasn't this beautiful in my former life. One particular day I was going to meet Cash Money Jay- which was the perfect name for him because he would regularly "cash out" 500 pounds or more every time he came through! One of the good things about dude was I never had to count his money. He always had it neatly arranged and was never a dollar short, the type of customers I fuck'n loved! I needed more of his type. Whenever he called, I was on my way!

I pulled up on Puritan and Linwood then backed up in the driveway in my van. I was greeted by his boys who came out to grab the bundles of weed. I got out, same routine as usual and walked to the front door while the two men took the bundles of weed through the side. On this particular day, I'm walking through the front door and to my surprise; I hear some scuffling on the side of the house! Before I could reach for my gun there was some nigga, who I couldn't make out right then. He came from behind me, on my heels with his gun against my head!

83

"BITCH! GETCHO ASS IN THE HOUSE!" The raspy voice of a guy yelled out!

It was then I realized I had made a bad move. One word popped in the back of my mind *"Checkmate."*

Again I was facing my fate. A vision of death came over me as I saw my life flash before my eyes!

"FUCK" they're about to rob and kill us!" I cried to myself!

So many things flashed thru my mind. I was gonna be another victim on Fox 2 news. I could see it now flashing across the screen "Breaking News". My parents will be hurt, my sister will not understand. Damn! I had an appointment with the bad side of the good life and there was nothing I could do about it. Not to mention this crazy muthafucka didn't have a mask on! He had this distinct look and his grill was filled with platinum! He had a Detroit accent too, so I knew he wasn't a country boy. But no mask? They may as well start printing the RIP T-shirts. Who do you know that lived through some shit like that?!

As we went further into the house I came upon three more unfamiliar faces and they all had guns too. One of them was standing on the wall near the front door and had an old school high-top fade. The other had these huge ass lips with this big nasty ass herpes looking sore on it. He stood in the middle of the floor looking at Cash Money Jay and the other two little niggas that unloaded the van. They must have hit the house from the front and the back. Damn, this was well planned because they surely had enough manpower for this shit, they was four deep. This C-Murder looking muthafucka was so black his eyes stood out. They were this jaundice yellow color looking sick as hell. He came in from the side door. I was trying to get a good look at these muthafuckas just in case I made it out of here alive! Cash Money Jay had more fear in his eyes than I had ever seen. I have been through some shit since I chose this lifestyle and career but I have never seen any man have that much fear in his face. All kind of shit was going through my head. What could I have done differently? I tried to replay the shit over and over again what could I have done to avoid this, as I was walked back to a room that was soon-to-be-bloodshed.

Why?! Why me?! Why now?! This is so fucked up!" I cried inside!

I was full of fear but I damn sure didn't show it like Cash Money Jay. The room was filled with some hungry ass goons with guns and us. We were helpless. They made the four of us sit on the couch as they pointed their guns at us constantly asking us about the whereabouts of the money!

"Yo dawg! Please don't kill me!" The little nigga near the wall pleaded.

The other little nigga on the other side of me cut him off!

"Fuck all this shit man, Yall can have that muthafuckn' money!, Let them have it Jay he begged! Ain't none of this shit worth dying for!" Cash Money Jay continued to plead with the niggas over and over, even offering them to take the weed, which was at least $500,000 worth of work!

Them niggas wasn't hearing that shit tho! I could tell they knew it was something better in the building. They wanted the *money* because it was hassle free. They didn't wanna carry a bunch of fuckin bundles out the house, and then have to take that shit to the streets and sell it. That alone would come with consequences and a lot of risk. They weren't new to this shit. Who's to say they wouldn't run into some of our people who they stole it from, and get laid the fuck out on the spot! Shit like that happens every day in the D. There weren't many people gettin' work in that amount anyway so it would be obvious to anyone who was familiar with me and my circle where that shit came from which in turn would bring pain to the game.

I looked at this hoe ass nigga and yelled out,

"Jay! Please give these nigga's the money baby please!"

The look on their face let me know this wasn't about any damn negotiations.

"These nigga's mean business so please give it to them or tell them where it is, shit I'm tryin to live," I begged mercifully.

Fuck a damsel in distress a bitch was scared and in a fucked up situation in the worst way ever. I wasn't ready to die over no penny-pushing-balling-backwards ass muthafucka! I had a whole life ahead of me and I was just starting to enjoy the shit! This Cash Money Jay muthafucka better give these goons whatever the fuck they wanted because I could see they were growing inpatient and it wasn't gonna be long before they started putting pressure on an already intense situation. This fool better get to stuffing them garbage bags with his dumb ass.

So the two little niggas were pleading with him while I'm pleading with him as well. We were all pleading for our lives trying to get this dumb ass nigga to give them what they came for. I was also thinking how none of the shit was worth my life! The way I move, it wouldn't have been a major loss any damn way! I would have the money and the weed back by the end of the month! It's nothing to a boss. I just knew I needed to be alive to make it happen.

We were scared as fuck shoulder to shoulder, knee to knee. I swear one of these niggas pissed they pants. I smelled it along with the fear from this hoe ass nigga. Cash Money Jay turned and looked over at me and cried out like a bitch,

"F! I swear it ain't no money in the house Ma! I'm not about to put us at risk like that baby-girl! Ain't shit here!"

Now to see this fool cry had me feeling some kinda way. I thought he was a nigga wit' some backbone, some muscle. If I had known I was dealing with a bitch-ass-nigga like this I would have *never* brought my ass over here by myself without some kinda backup. Niggas true colors come out under pressure. I'm looking at this nigga knowing he got to be lying because something was completely wrong with this picture. If there was no money in this muthafuckin house then *how the fuck was he gonna pay me*???!! My thug ass got mad instantly. At that point I just wanted to pay these goons to let me go and off this nigga! It was then when I saw RED! I was so ready to pull some kind of MacGyver move right then! I swear it became a do-or-die moment for me.

The goon with the big herpes lip appeared to be the leader. He pulled his gun out from his hip as he walked to Cash Money Jay, put it to his head and cocked it. This is the end, I thought to myself as I began to pray to God for an immediate miracle.

"You got 10 seconds nigga!" He said gritting his teeth.

"LOOK MAN I SWEAR ON MY KIDS I AIN'T GOT SHIT IN HERE!" Jay cried out.

"Ten..." He started counting down.

"SEARCH THE HOUSE! LOOK IN EVERY ROOM! I WOULDN'T LIE TO YALL DAWG! Jay was sweating and pleading.

"Nine." He continued counting like Jay hadn't said a word.

"PLEASE MAN PLEASE ITS NOT WORTH IT" Jay wasted his breath.

The guy just kept counting down; he had the last ten seconds of this niggaz life in his hands. We all sat there helplessly waiting on them to blow his brains out all over us and then kill the rest of us one by one! I already knew what was next, I seen it in the movies too many times. Cash Money Jay got on his knees and begged the guy to spare him from death; he was down to the last five seconds and counting. I turned my head away and closed my eyes because in those last critical seconds, the only thing you have left is a few moments of prayer. I could hear the other goon laughing yelling out,

"KILL THAT LYING ASS BITCH! THAT FUCK BOY HOLDING BACK OVER THERE CRYING LIKE A PUSSY ASS NIGGA! FUCK EM!" The one with the platinum grill said sounding anxious to kill him and be done with it.

Me and the other two little niggas damn near in unison screaming,

"PLEASE! PLEASE! COME ON JAY! TELL THEM WHERE THE FUCKIN MONEY IS!"

Knowing this nigga knew more than what he was telling these dudes! We were all sitting shoulder to shoulder on this raggedy ass couch with springs sticking me all up in my ass! I was damn near ready to die from the discomfort alone! What the fuck have I got myself into? I pushed for one last opportunity for this clown to give these heartless fools what they wanted. Shit still ain't work!

The final two seconds of his life had finally arrived when I heard the guy holding the gun to his head say,

"Two…"

That's when this nigga Jay yelled out,

"OKAY! OKAY! WAIT! I GOT YOU! JUST DON'T SHOOT ME!"

This stupid ass nigga been playing with my life all this time. He held his hand up in a shielding gesture to block a possible bullet impact in case the gun went off.

I opened my eyes and turned back to look at him on the floor looking up to the dude holding the gun. To my surprise this nigga pulled about $12,000 out his pocket and said this is all the cash he had on him! I just kept looking back and forth between the Goons and Cash Money Jay. It seemed like time itself had stopped. In that small moment of silence, I watch him snatch the money from him and toss it over to the platinum grill nigga that walked my ass in. That seemed to calm his anxious ass down for a minute though. He retreated across the room as if he was waiting for his next order. These niggas had this all planned out, this was not a practice run for they ass. They all had guns and had every door and window covered. They have most definitely done this before, which fucked me up even more.

I don't know exactly how to explain what I was feeling right then, but it made a light bulb go on in my head. I noticed something that was a little strange, whoever this goon was with this ugly ass high top fade, knew Cash Money Jay by his nickname. I heard him say it! I guess I set off some kind of intensity in the room with the expression on my face. It was evident that I must have realized something that I shouldn't have. The Herpes Lip goon looked over at me, and then slowly turned his head to look down on the floor at Cash Money Jay with the gun still focused on him. It was if he had an epiphany. Somehow he too figured something was just not right. Within seconds he turned the gun off Cash Money Jay and shot the goon with the old school high-top fade. This nigga was here with him, or so I thought. I really didn't know what the fuck was going on. I almost shitted on myself because what part of the fucking horror film is this? His nasty lip ass shot his own dude dead smack-center between the eyes. Blood splattered everywhere! This infested lip muthafucka switched lanes with no blinkers right before my eyes! I don't think anybody in the room seen that coming. I lost it! I felt so weak seeing that shit happen right before my eyes, I could barely keep my head up. Cash Money Jay had this look on his face that kept changing throughout the entire time. As if he was suddenly taken by surprise or something. I knew we were in a fucked up situation but his expressions let me know there was more to this shit. I couldn't really read every expression though because I was still focused on whether I was going to live or die at that moment. It seemed like it took forever for the goon's lifeless body to fall limp and hit the floor. His head hit the floor last and his body shook two times. I stared at the puddle of blood that started to form on the dirty wood floors. I just knew I was next. It was at that moment I realized something had really gone wrong. Cash Money Jay stared at the guy who had the fade with a sense of sadness in his eyes; he looked down and said,

"Follow me to the safe".

At this point I am beyond the state of confusion. This nigga had gone from begging and pleading for his life to *follow me to the safe* after swearing that there was no money in the house! I knew something was strange, but again when you got a bunch of ugly ass black niggas with guns attempting to rob and kill you, you have a tendency to pay more attention to a way to escape without being killed, than other shit going on around you.

They ordered me and Cash Money Jay to get off the couch together, while the two little niggas sat shaking in their boots. They already knew they couldn't leave my ass unattended. Now there were still four of these muthafuckas I had to keep my eyes on. Them *and* Cash Money Jay because he was clearly a part of the original plan to take my work. Platinum Teeth accompanied Herpes Lip as Cash Money Jay took them to this safe. Yellow jaundice eyes that was now watching me, motioned me to go too as he followed a few feet behind, gun in hand. They tried to walk ahead and whisper, but I could hear damn near everything they were saying. Cash Money Jay leaned into dude whispering,

"What the fuck was that you just did back there Nigga you killed my mans DAMN! Ain't nobody told yo' ass to shoot nobody! And now you asking for my money?! The deal was to have baby girl come thru and get the weed! Fuck you mean *where is the money?* What part of the deal was that?" Cash Money Jay questioned with fear in his voice.

It was in that moment some of the suspicion I was having in the living room became real. Now the whole thing started to make a lot of sense to me. The pieces of the puzzle were slowly coming together. All of these niggas was in on the hit on me, but this Herpes lip muthafucka had a plan B for all our asses. Herpes lip began waving his gun with aggression in his voice,

"Nigga shut the fuck up! I'm doing things my way! And if you haven't noticed by now BITCH, I'm the nigga holding the gun and as you can see I don't have a problem using it! That was yo' peoples and I couldn't stand his punk ass anyway. Nigga had too much fuckin mouth. He was plotting to get your ass after this hit and was gonna split that shit with me. I wasn't splitn' shit wit' his hoe ass, shit if he flipped on you he will flip on me too. He had to go. Now... you gotta problem with that?!" Herpes Lip snapped!

Cash Money Jay knew right then whatever the initial plot was had turned on his ass! That's also when I realized I wasn't getting out of there alive. It was way too much shit in the game to allow me to just walk away free. I began to wonder what additional plans they had for me. Imagine waiting to die with visions of your life continuously flashing with each blink of your eyes. My family is gonna be in so much pain, I never wanted to hurt them. Damn how did I let my guard down? I remembered my gun was still in my purse, they never even searched me. But I damn sure wasn't going to try and go for it because they asses had a few sets of eyes on me. Fuck being superwoman at this point, I had to use my Lois Lane brain and try to figure my way out and not wrapped up in some carpet. I'm thinking like a muthafucka.

We slowly walked into the room where the safe was supposed to be. I couldn't believe I was walking to my death with some Nikes on, clutching my Gucci bag against my stomach. The walls were yellow and the paint was cracked. The floors were wood and made a creaking noise with every step, just like the scene in a horror film. There was a bathroom on the left, another room on the right. Herpes Lip pushed Cash Money Jay into the last door on the left, as if he knew where to go any way. He had been here or somebody had told him. He let Jay lead the way but this nigga knew where it was anyway, I could tell. Just like I was fully aware he was not new to this shit. We are at the point of no return I told myself.

My frightened body stopped just short of entering this fucked up ass room that smelled like ass and feet! Platinum mouth stood near the window which must have been cracked open because the draft frequently pushed an extra dose of the funky smell right past my nose. The odor was thick, strong enough to disappear in. Yellow jaundice eyes watched over me as we stood with one foot in and the other outside the room. His eyes were blank and moved back and forth from me and the two little niggas shitting on themselves on the couch. He seemed unbothered by everything, as if he played this role often. I knew my looks couldn't save me from this shit, if anything it made it worse. I could tell by how they were looking at me. They may try to rape my ass before they off me. I admit I was nervous as hell having to endure all of this turmoil and chaos, but through it all I was still well aware of my surroundings, steadily trying to figure out my next move.

I kept my head straight ahead but moved my eyes to see what was going on without being noticeable. I noticed the safe partially covered under some stained ass dirty draws and old Coney Island containers around it. Cash Money Jay was stumbling over clothes and a nasty funky mattress that was on the floor kicking shit off to the side to create a path to the safe. As soon as he got in arms reach of the safe, the Herpes lip goon put the gun right to Jay's head and said, "Now open this goddamn safe before I place a bullet in yo' head, BITCH!" His aggressive tone proved he meant business and whatever previous agreement they had was currently null and void.

"So this is how it is? This ain't how we planned this shit man! I thought we were good dawg?!" He pleaded one last time with the chrome to his dome.

"It's up to you..." He said playing with his gun, licking his infested ass lip and looking over at me treacherously and said, "You got a lot of foul people around you man. I knew about the safe before I even got here". He turned his attention to me.

His stare made me even more uneasy. I knew I was a part of his plan to end this murder mystery. I was already fighting the cold sweats and numb feeling in my feet as I stood in silence. I swear I checked to see if I pissed my pants a few times.

Herpes Lip continued the stare saying, "You can try and be superman if you want to, fuck around and die never knowing who dropped the dime on your dumb ass, then I will just stick my dick in that pretty ass bitch right there and then smoke her ass right afterwards. Or... and there is an or... you can do the smart thing by opening that safe and then you can keep yours and this pretty bitch life. It's up to you, and my patience is growing thin muthafucka!!" I knew this nigga had sex on his mind. Whoever would have thought the same pretty face that opened so many doors for me was gonna be the reason I died horribly. He didn't want to just kill my ass but he wanted to fuck me too. At that point I knew Cash Money Jay sorry ass was gonna die regardless and he deserved it because he set me up, but then that meant I was next! All that was keeping us alive was some extra gangsta shit that came from watching too much fucking TV! These niggas wasn't amateurs and something had to give. It was kill or be killed at that very moment! I had made up in my mind that I somehow was going to fight for my life. In that same thought I put my head down, slightly closed my eyes and began to pray for a way out. That's when to my surprise I heard gunshots! POW! POW! POW! My eyes popped open, the wheels in my mind turned even faster. It was like slow motion. Jaundice eyes turned around for a millisecond which was all the time needed to reach for my steel, a pink 9mm and I just started letting loose.

Shots went ballistic as I turned my head away not knowing where the bullets landed and didn't give a fuck! The little niggas looked like they saw Jesus when they seen me stumble from the door way blazing. I backed out the doorway still shooting and trying to make my way to the exit. I could hear the front door slam open as I lost my balance. My back hit the wall in the hallway as I pushed Jaundice eyes to the floor. His ugly ass was laid out gasping for air, blood fucking everywhere! I quickly got my balance and headed down the hallway to the door holding my gun in an aimed position not giving a fuck about nothing other than getting my ass out of there like them two little niggas did! Luckily this particular day I wasn't in my stilettos, my Air Max made my exit a lot easier. I ran out the opened door fumbling for my keys. Just when I thought I was in the clear, platinum teeth ran out behind me letting loose from inside the house! POW! Ting! Bing! The bullets ricocheted off the gate as he grew closer. "AUHHHH!" I screamed dodging bullets jumping into my van, nervously turning the ignition, dropping that bitch in drive, and screeched off! It was like a scene out of a movie. He was obviously injured causing him to lose speed and not be as close up on me as he should have been! I sped off like my life depended on it, shit my life did depend on it. I ducked down as bullets riddled my back window. It seemed like I was caught in a nightmare! After being shot at, no one could have told me I wasn't dreaming! I was still wondering who in the hell made it out besides the two little niggas and this grill having muthafucka that was determined to get a hold of my ass. I began to thank the Lord for saving me from myself. I knew I had slipped and it could have meant death, the thought had tears pouring out my eyes. I began to pray out loud soon as I got off that block.

14

"Ignorance Is Bliss"

Ignorance is bliss. I would hear that phrase from time to time and it had this ring to it that fascinated me, but I never really saw how it played a role in my life until I escaped death after a robbery gone bad. You know, I live by the moment. Of course I would hear the stories about niggas in the streets being robbed and killed over drugs, jealousy and all kind of vindictive day-by-day shit. Like many that smoke knowing it causes cancer, those of us who have sex without protection knowing the risk of venereal diseases and something even worse, HIV/AIDS, we live by the moment. We take risks everyday knowing we may not survive long enough to learn from its consequence. I say all of this to say, all the material shit, the money, the balling ass niggas in the world cannot replace the air I breathe. This is something I have always held steadfast to but it wasn't until I was facing death that I realized how much danger I was in, daily. I have to find my way if I want to overcome the evil in the world. I dodged a bullet that could have claimed my life! I was lucky to have escaped under the circumstances! I was alive and well, and ready to get to the muthafuckin bottom of how the shit jumped off, costing me more than what I was willing to forget about.

I couldn't believe what had just happened! *I SHOT THAT NIGGA!* I stared out the window as I thought to myself, smiling at the thought of him possibly being dead! Better him than me. It was obvious when the first gun was pulled out someone was going to die! But who in the hell was responsible for this? Why did Cash Money have me in the middle of this mess? Then who was it that changed the script because even Jay didn't see it coming. Then again why was he stalling when he was down from the beginning? I was counting my questions and my blessings at the same time.

After leaving Sinai Grace, the hospital known for niggas who go in and don't come out, I knew if I made it this far I was not gonna let these nurses and doctors cut my shit short. My body was sore, but I'd live. I was ready to roll up and roll the fuck out! So much on my mind, I couldn't stop smoking. I don't drink but I needed a fifth of the strongest shit from the top shelf. I just couldn't believe this nigga Cash Money Jay would play me like that! I helped that nigga get rich! I mean I had been serving dude for years! I wonder why he chose to do this now? He must have been plotting on me, and I had no idea. Karma is a bitch because herpes lip leaked some info too. Someone else had flipped on Cash Money Jay, other than the dead nigga in the living room. Why me tho? I couldn't understand it. My mind was spinning with thoughts of that day's events. It was haunting me. Everyone in my path reminded me of them niggas. But the biggest thing I wondered about was who survived in that backroom. I still couldn't help but wonder if Cash was laying there bleeding to death. One thing for sure, his ass better had died if he knew what the fuck I knew. I was trying to stick around the hospital to see who made it out alive and learned that one of the goons ended up making it! The one that tried to run out behind me ended up gettting shot and I got word within moments that he knew who put it all together. I couldn't wait to look this man in the eyes like nigga who sent you? I wanted to know the details of his failed plans to end my life. I needed to know.

I went to the crib, got in touch with a few of my contacts to update them on what just happened. I wasn't sure what was next, so I had to let my peeps know the latest. I felt an unusual sense of urgency, as if I was number one on the jackers list and they was gunning for me. I felt like I was being haunted because I wasn't sure who made it out alive. I felt uneasy so I changed up my appearance and made my way back over to Sinai to holler at the survivor. I was on the edge but I also needed some answers.

I slid through all security and medical staff that was supposedly watching dude closely. I had that innocent look that made shit like this come easy. They just knew I was somebody's wife or something. Gently closing the door behind me, I stepped quietly towards the bed as he lay on his side facing the opposite way. I got up on him and leaned into his ass with vengeance resting my elbows on his jugular. I could tell he thought his life was over. He didn't waste any time telling me without hesitation who the driving force was behind this.

"It was that nigga Boogie" he said in his shaky voice. "He knew Cash Money Jay was gonna hit a lick on you so he sent his boy Chris with the fade instead. All along he had back doored Jay to get over on you and him at the same time."

Well I'd be damned. This was Cash Money Jay's right hand man! Dude went on begging me to leave him out of it saying he had nothing to do with it! *Oh really?* Well by the looks of it, he appeared to be looking like a have-something-to-do-with-it nigga to me! Something told me to let him live and get to the real bottom of this shit so I did. I reached out to a few people I trusted, just so they won't be next. Nobody knew anything and the streets was not talking. Where is this nigga Boogie? Did Cash Money Jay make it? I had so many questions as my mind wandered. I changed up my moves and remained cautious, not knowing what to expect. A few days went past, no new news. Things changed rapidly, and the streets suddenly turned into a war zone for five days straight. DPD was not prepared, it was like baby Iraq. Violence filled the city, shootouts, drive by's, people coming up missing, houses fire bombed, cars too. I stayed in the house after the second day of the madness. Just laid up in my plush bed nestled in my white down covers with plenty of weed, Garcia Vegas and snacks. I'm flipping through the channels while keeping my eye on my four security cameras, blazing. I had put word out there how a muthafucka tried me, so I most definitely was laying low.

My phone rang. It was my homey from 7 mile telling me to hurry up and turn on the news. I clicked on channel 4 and it was in the middle of a Breaking News alert. They flashed the pictures of five people in connection to a murder scene on Detroit's west side. The smoke filled the air as the glare from the TV illuminated the room. I inhaled so deep I just wanted to help my mind grasp what I just seen. There was a mini war in the city and within weeks *everybody* and I mean EVERY-MUTHAFUCKIN-BODY that was in that house that day was in a body bag with a toe tag. Everybody except me, the two little niggas and the goon that gave me the info. Everyone else was DEAD! What in the fuck is really going on? My mind raced even faster than ever now. Phone still in my hand, mouth wide open, ashes staining my pearly white sheets. I was stuck. Was I experiencing the power that automatically came with the money and the respect? I felt a sense of relief and satisfaction of some sort. I hit the blunt again and began to wonder. Who is taking responsibility for this? Is this retaliation from some other dumb shit they did or is this directly related to my night of horror? Then I unselfishly relished in the thought of them being taught a lesson.

It was after that experience, I decided to change a few things in my life. I became a little more cold hearted, and to some it affected my relationships but most of all the people I did business with. It became a situation where I didn't know who to trust. Shit was so bad I wouldn't even date. I was spooked that the nigga might try and set me up! I felt like everybody had bad intentions but I wasn't going to risk my life trying to figure it out. I started back-peddling. I needed someone solid. I needed to feel secure. I found myself back to dating Will again. This was a mental challenge when dealing with him though. Trust was a huge issue between us when it came to his hoes. But when it came to my life, real shit, I knew for sure Will had my back!

Speaking of...*my back...he introduced me to what* just happened to be one of my favorite positions, legs closed and on my back. He loved caressing my long legs; I always gave him all the good loving he needed whenever he needed it. Every day was like the first time and that meant *good as hell*. I can remember one particular time

101

this nigga was going in on the pussy. The way he sucked on my clit had me purring like a kitten. My nipples got so hard as he embraced me pinning my pussy down with the opening of his mouth dropping his tongue deep down into my tight tunnel of love. I could feel a stream of his saliva falling in between the crack of my ass that was *soooo* wet. Like when I sucked his dick, he would love the way I allowed this overwhelming amount of moisture from my mouth to make this smacking noise and that turned him on major. Our sex life was deeper than the Atlantic. We had side bitch issues from time to time but overall, I loved everything about this man. Not just the things he did for me before he got locked up. Our sexual chemistry created a crazy connection. It was something deeper than both of our pockets. It was magical, full of excitement, I'm talking good love making, and I fulfilled his every fantasy. I laugh now thinking about how freaky I was. I was a total package, which was one of the reasons why I couldn't see the nigga looking anywhere else, it just didn't make sense! I was stuck and fucked with this homie lover friend. The head game, off the chain on both ends. This nigga deserved *the eating pussy of the nile* award! Lying on my back with my ass up in the air fighting for that nut that was forcing its way down into his mouth.

"*Fuck iz'shu doing to me...*" I moaned out as I grabbed the back of his head pulling him into me with one hand and played with my nipple with the other.

"*Mmmm...*" He grunted as to say how much he enjoyed the way I tasted.

I tried to smother his ass with these fat pussy lips that clawed against the outskirts of his mouth. I was so into it. A bitch was in the zone rocking my hips like I was up for *Best AZZSTRESS!* He could feel me trembling down there. The more intense it was the more he snuggled against me. I have had head in the past and them niggas didn't really know what the fuck they was doing! This one was different, and different was what had my ass caught up in his spider's web. I loved him before, but at this point I was deeply in love, a bitch head was gone, nose wide open. I often pondered on ways to ever repay him; somehow I knew one day I would be able to give him something to show my deep love for him. I'll worry about that later because I knew I was falling in love with hopes that he was ready to catch me. Although falling in love was not a part of the plan, this was the effect he had on me. He knew all my weak spots. Right when I was vulnerable. He knew when I needed someone to comfort me with all I had been through. When I needed someone who knew me well and loved me before I made my stamp in the streets. He was that and more, he made me feel safe and secure. Furthermore, he was different now, than when we were together before he did his bid.

We went deeper than other men from my past. I had a very close bond with his daughter, and I always kept in contact with her even through his bid. Before I knew it, Will and I started spending everyday together. It wasn't long before I let him move in with me on this *'Baby I'm going to prove I can be loyal'* tip. Knowing he had a side bitch issue, but after all I been through I wanted to take a chance on love ... With Will. I ain't gonna' lie the dick was lovely but that fact itself was a constant reminder that *these hoes ain't loyal!* He was on a roll and I was enjoying every moment of it. I felt protected when I was with him. He *had* my best interest at heart and it felt good. Will was rubbing it on so thick that I found myself falling even more and deeper in love, letting my guard down, all the way down.

That one important rule Mrs. King tried to instill in me when I was younger, *"The one who loves the least controls the relationship"* got thrown out the window hell I was in love! I fell into this head first. I mean this was the man who purchased my first place, furnished it, bought me lavish jewelry and took me on elegant trips to places I never knew existed on this planet! So I felt now that the table had kind of turned and I was getting money I didn't mind returning the favor. I felt like I owed him. Will was the first person I actually told how much money I had! Going against my better judgment, I totally ignored what O told me. Thinking back on one of our late night drives.

"F, never let the right hand know what the left hand is doing!" He told me

"Why baby?" I questioned rhetorically.

I knew what the hell he meant; I just used to love listening to his lectures. He looked at me with this crazy expression like, bitch you couldn't be that stupid, and then said something so powerful that only a man with that kind of influence would say.

"The best secret is within self."

"*Hmmmm...* I like that."

"I want you to love that. Embrace that knowledge baby girl." He said lying back in his plush'd leather seat lighting a cigar with this Rick Ross swag he had.

Though they look nothing alike, O put me in the mind of one of those high profiled rappers. Their demeanor, the way they talk, walk. O was all of that minus the microphone. His confidence made me feel like I had just left a round table with the Godfather. I couldn't say nothing but,

"I got you O." I winked making my way out the door to hit up the mall.

This time it seemed like he was telling me for a direct reason but I kept it moving. I wouldn't say what he said was ignored. I was just moving really fast with all the money I was making. I thought there really wasn't much he could have told me that I didn't already know then. I was so wrong and should'a listened more closely.

Back at the house, I grabbed Will's hand.

"Lemme show you something baby" I said with a devilish grin on my face.

Will followed me like a puppy, curious to see what I had in store. I opened the closet door and parted my clothes to view the back wall. In full view was a safe that both me and Will could sit in comfortably. I turned the knob entering the combination and opened the door to the safe. Sitting in front view was my money counter. Behind it sat rows and rows of money in stacks that I had separated by rubber bands in 10 thousand bundles. Will was in shock! The only words he could utter right then was,

"GAWWWDAMN!"

He couldn't believe it!! I wanted him to see that we didn't need to focus on another nigga's money and connects when I had already had my own.

"We in this together baby. What's yours is mine and what's mine is mine" I joked.

We inhaled the moment as we laid back on my rich Dubai carpet, I had custom ordered from one of the richest countries in the world! I wanted the best of everything, and never once doubted having it. I was destined for greatness and I was determined to always reach for more.

I think that money made his dick hard or something. It was like he had took some Viagra. We was on some rock star shit. Fucking all over the lower level, pulling bands out of the safe making it rain on his ass, we was on some real high shit. The weed was good, we had the music blasting, and a bitch was in the zone! Then suddenly Will stops and asked,

"So just to be clear", Will must have been thinking of a master plan and fucking and sucking at the same damn time, "is this yours?"

I kind of gave him this crazy look as if to say, "why the fuck would I have another nigga's money in my muthafuckin safe and not be with the dude whose money it is!" Why the fuck would I be sitting up in my crib with Will's ass is what I'm sayin'! Niggas be sayin' some of the dumbest shit sometimes, but I guess in some situations when your dealing with a regular bitch with no conscience better safe than sorry. He needed clarification, I could respect that because that's how these street dudes get set up, and some killed! These hood-rats out here be trying to get money by using niggas saying the shit they got is theirs when in reality, the money, jewelry, cars and cribs was financed through some cat they den' turned out! This can bring unnecessary problems to the table a muthafucka don't need. Niggas get killed over shit like that, so when he asked that question in a more playful way, in the back of my mind, I figured he was probably being more safe than sorry. I wasn't trippin'. I loved this black ass nigga to death, and at that point I would do almost anything for his ass. So I replied in my sexy voice,

"Naw baby this right here is *OURS!*"

The look on his face was priceless! He had the information he needed to finalize his mental master plan. That nigga was happier than a gay guy in a room filled with dicks LOL! We were what people in the streets called a *power couple*. I hadn't changed up much at all but he was finally free and ready to get busy. I was still cautious though, so I still had my same road-dawgs that would help me bag up pounds of dope. I remember one day me and my home-girls was sitting around my European marble table packing up some shit and before we started packing up I yelled out slapping my hands down on the table,

"YO! Y'all bitches need to strip!"

They all looked at me like I was on something crazy as the room that was filled with noise and laughter suddenly came to a halt.

"Bitch, *whaat* the fuck!" Robin squinted her eyes looking over at me with a drink in one hand and a blunt in the other.

"Y'all bitches strip! I want titties hanging, and ass's swanging! Y'all bitches ain't about to pack up shit if I can't make sure I can trust you with my shit!" I pointed at all of them in a back and forth gesturing motion.

Tamara said, "Hoe this ain't New Jack City!" She laughed.

Robin looked in between us both and said, "And bitch you damn sho' ain't no Nino Brown!"

I just fell out laughing at all they ass! We always had crazy moments when I just say anything and they have to determine if it's real or if I'm just bullshittin. They been around me so long they knew 99 % of the time I was bullshittin. They started throwing money at me and shit. It

107

was one of the moments that we will always remember, I always get they ass!

Me and my money team hung out every other day, and it wasn't long before I was adding horses to my stable. See the term 'horse to my stable' is viewed different from how men portray it. These 'horses' are my home-girls and in my world I pick my breed of friends like a four-leaf clover. I was choosy because bitches are dirty like niggas. Jealousy and greed is not gender biased. I only fucked with a selected few. I don't misuse the word 'friends' and I don't use that shit loosely! Will was also selective about the company he kept, that's another thing I like about him. One of his boys had a girlfriend named Tia that eventually became one of my ride or dies! Overtime she proved her loyalty and love. And she always made me laugh. I never knew she would become one of my best friends.

The days went by and the seasons changed. Michigan weather is so unpredictable. We can have on swimsuits Monday and be snowboarding Tuesday, you just never know. One thing that became consistent was the time Will and I spent together. You never seen me without Will and you never seen Will without Fauna. Sam and Tia were usually with us also. In our world where you live everyday like your last we treated personal appearances as if we were celebrities. It didn't matter if the location was a McDonald's on a day when we just looking for a quick fix to hold us over! We got the goons! We kept at least four of them with us at *all* times. They were guys Will trusted an' grew up with. Friend or no friend, business was business and we paid them well to play the roles they played. I couldn't go to the bathroom without these niggaz!

It was a good feeling to hang out with friends and surround ourselves with those we considered on our level and feel safe.

Shit was subject to change in our world on a daily basis, so we had to be prepared for it. We lived like rock stars and we were the hood celebrities. We had to switch up things often, even things like never rockn' the same thing twice. Nothing that went on from the time we woke up til the time we laid down was ever done the same. That was one thing about the two everyone called Detroit's Power Couple. Our routine changed which made it hard for onlookers to know our next move. Only those who were closest to us would know our most intimate secrets - mistake number muthafuckn' one.

Never in a million years would me and Will have ever thought we would find out that those same muthafukas we called friends and family would be those same muthafuckas we would end up having to watch our back from. We learned to trust no one. Keep family and close friends on deck only. It's always been rules and levels to this shit. I know I needed to be more careful with my appearance, especially after the setup, but fuck all that I always shined bright like a diamond before I had diamonds! If I wanted to buy my man $600,000 worth of jewelry, that was my fuckin prerogative! I love to shop and I love to spoil my man and friends! That was just something I loved to do when dollars was rolling in like that! Hell, you only live once. I had it and I was damn sho' gon' spend it. A wise man once said, "You may as well spend it because you can't take it with you anyway".

Will could get it in many ways: the pussy, the diamonds, house and cars, I loved the shit out of that no-good black muthafucka I swear to Gawd! Platinum Rolex masterpiece iced all the way out, gold and rose gold Rolexes, a *Jacob* watch, diamond chains, bracelets and most of all, a wedding ring to match every set. That's right! I said it! We were going to elope ASAP! It couldn't get no deeper than this. Will was the man I wanted to spend the rest of my life with so a few months later we were married! Our name was ringing in the streets about the Mister and Missus. I mean we looked like superstars riding thru the D. We were the *Jay-Z* and *Beyonce* couple of Detroit! Will had the Benz and Range and I had this gorgeous deep red Lexus on red spinners and the supped up Hummer. We were living like the people on TV and in the magazines. Of course as to be expected, not everybody liked that shit. With all this glamour shit, you know what came next, another brave muthafucka wit' balls wanting to try us.

15

"Do or Die"

Everything you do in life has some type of consequence, some worse than others. I knew early on the consequences of my beautiful hustle, but that did not stop me. Now that I was with Will, the rumors flew away and any nigga on the street knew not to try me. But there was an incident where two guys broke into Tia and Sam's crib and held them at gunpoint demanding their weed and money. LaSalle was the trap. We all chilled there. A lot of our shit was stored there and everything in between. The night when that fucked up shit went down with Tia and Sam happened to be the eve of Thanksgiving. Will and I had put everything down early because we were tired as hell. Not to mention everybody else had left also. Will and I were always the life of the party, so when we left, all the entertainment left with us.

Anyways, Sam and Tia were living on LaSalle at the time. They were the only two left in this gigantic ass house, when we bounced on this particular night. It was my understanding that while these hoe ass niggas were breaking in through a window on the first floor, Tia and Sam were asleep upstairs. Tia slept like a muthafucka in a deep coma, and Sam, always slept with one eye open. I guess on this night everyone had a little too much to drink and smoke, because while they were getting their beauty rest, the goons were creeping through their shit picking up everything they saw that they could liquidate. We talking AK-47s, an AR-15 and Sam's right hand piece he would never leave home without - his Glock 45.

These niggas kicked in the bedroom door bringing both Tia and Sam to their knees yelling out, "SHOW ME YOUR MUTHAFUCKIN HANDS NOW!"

Sam couldn't really make out what was happening because it was dark as hell, and the only light was what was piercing through their bedroom window from the dim streetlights. They immediately came to the realization that these ignorant ready-to-die muthafuckas wasn't bullshittin, and they were willing to comply with whatever they had to do to get out of the situation alive. Guns were pointed at their heads and one of the robbers yelled out,

"NIGGA LAY DOWN ON THE FLOOR AND BITCH YOU KEEP YOUR HANDS UP AND LAY ON TOP OF HIM!" Tia was crying and following every demand.

She slowly laid on top of him as they requested. Sam, on the other hand was irritable, which could have gotten them both killed at any moment. That was the kind of nigga he was though, a hot head, pissed because they were violating him and his women. Tia knew this, and begged him to stay cool. Knowing he was one that would go out with a fight even if he had to choose between him or them, she whispered in his ear "baby stay cool we gone make it out of here alive," as she pressed her lips against his back. Her hands grasped his forearms as she prayed for their lives to be spared.

"BITCH! SHUT THE FUCK UP AND GET BOTH YALL ASSES FACE DOWN ON THE FLOOR BEFORE

I SMOKE YALL MUTHAFUCKAS!" One of the robbers snapped.

He was one of those trigger-happy niggas that was looking for a reason to plant a bullet in the back of their heads. Sam had enough and snapped back. All the shit talking back and forth along with the chaos was causing a lot of ruckus. So while Tia was keeping her eyes on the chrome against her dome, Sam was on some fuck y'all nigga shit! Sam eventually submitted to the robber's demands as they got off the floor and prepared for the duct tape and tie up process. Neither one of them knew how their nightmare would end. While Tia and Sam laid helplessly on their bedroom floor, the robbers moved on with what their initial plan was setup to do. Tia couldn't stop praying which was bringing some sense of peace to what was going on, while Sam on the other hand was thinking of a master plan which in turn may get them both killed if it was not orchestrated properly. The way the robbers had them laid out meant only one thing to Sam... execution style!! Hell, THIS IS DETROIT and niggas on this kind of shit almost *never* leave witnesses to come back and haunt them in the end! Why else would they have been tied up face down!

"WHERE IS THE MONEY AND THE DOPE?" One of the robbers kicked Sam in his side letting him know he meant business.

Tia cried out nervously, "I have twenty-five hundred in my purse and he should have about five thousand in a plastic bag in that closet with at least thirteen bows next to it! PLEASE! JUST TAKE THAT SHIT AND LET US GO!!" Tia pleaded.

Short of breath, and trying to speak out after the hard hit to his right rib cage by a nigga in some Timberland boots,

Sam said, "Wha...what the fuck Tia! No matter what we give these niggas they ain't letting us go! You gotta think Ma!" he robber kicked his foot back and into his side rib cage again!

"Shut the fuck up you bitch ass nigga and let the lady talk!

"PLEASE! Just take it all and let us live!!" Tia pleaded for both their lives one last time after giving up all the leverage she had to possibly bargain with these fools!

The robbers scuffled through the drawers and all kind of shit looking for everything they could possibly find that would have guaranteed more than enough capital for them all to split. Surprisingly, they grabbed that shit fast as hell, ran out the door and never looked back! They made it out of there with well over $20,000! They didn't even need them little 22s they came in with. After cleaning up and taking inventory, it was discovered that they actually left them there. They were both lucky to have survived this shit fa-real! I mean, come on! They got robbed with their own damn guns! How fucked up was that!

After this, we all vowed to never leave our guns out everywhere on some drunk night shit. That was when I knew Tia was a muthafuckn G! The bitch knew where the $250,000 stash was and never once led them niggas to it!

She was risking a lot by giving them those pennies! So while Sam thought Tia was showing signs of weakness by crying and pleading for their lives, the bitch had her own master plan already laid out while Sam laid there helplessly thinking of one. This is when she officially earned her spot on the team. Pressure burst pipes but pressure also makes diamonds. Clearly Tia was a diamond from the rough ass projects. Even scared and under pressure, she played her part. Not only did she show me her loyalty, she proved to me she wasn't what Sam obviously thought she was - soft as cotton. Not too many women are built for this lifestyle. But my BFF *Mz. Tia* was as gangsta as her girl who walked beside her! She was and still is my Bitch for life.

16"

"The Little Green Man on my Shoulder"

Sitting in my Jacuzzi tub, bubbles covering my body. My scented candle filled the room. I was loving every moment of it. In my line of work relaxing does not come often. The warm water relaxed my body, because my mind has been in a race for the last few days. *Was it a sign? Was my mind forcing me to reflect on past experiences and conversations for a purpose? Was I about to be in a position to have to use these lessons? Was I unconsciously preparing myself for some shit to pop off? Was my gut telling me to prepare for some shady shit?* I was not sure where these thoughts and feelings came from. I slid a little deeper in the water, the bubbles up to my neck and the end of my ponytail submerged in the water. I couldn't stop thinking about how shady niggas are. I closed my eyes as I went down memory lane.

It's so fucked up how people come into your life and you don't really know what their intentions are until it's too late. I think it's important to always reflect on those who came in and out of my life throughout this journey, whether they impacted me in a positive or negative way. Their presence played a role in my life, some way, somehow. Many played different parts like pieces in a puzzle in the development of my lifestyle, and though this nigga named Mason was a different type of cat that I wouldn't usually fuck wit', his fast-talking, slick ass was one I couldn't leave out of my story if I wanted to! I closed my eyes as I began to reminisce on a few things. Mason lived around the corner from me in my middle school days, and we were cool at least I thought. I would notice how he would always try to come around, but there was something I didn't trust about dude. My gut sensed his shade. This nigga would steal a right shoe from one store and the left shoe from another and come sell'em to me! Some crack head shit! Now tell me how one could trust a petty ass nigga like that!

When Will and I got back together after he got home, we kept running into dude. He would always try and small talk his way into our lives but I wasn't buying it. So this one particular day Mason caught Will out by himself and asked for his number so they could conduct some business. Will thought he was cool because I went to school with him. But wait - so if one of my- kindergarten teachers stepped to you and told you I was one of his favorite students and said *'Can you front me 50 bows'* you would do it nigga? I thought that was one of the craziest reasons to trust a muthafucka based off of a past relationship from middle school. I swear, sometimes Will made me wonder.

But anyways, so I'm chilling on the block one day smoking some *Indian Redd Byrd* (something one of my girls brought back from Africa with some balling ass nigga she was fucking wit') and I damn near choked when I saw Mason ass pull up on Will to get a package! Before I could pass the blunt I was on that nigga heels!

"WHOA WHOA WILL! WHY YOU FUCKIN WITH THAT NIGGA!"

I know I was loud as hell, but right then at that very

moment I didn't give a fuck. Hell! This was our livelihood and a bitch could never be too careful when it came to fucking wit' some random ass niggas, whether I knew them or not. I had been through too much to play too loose like this. There was a process one would have to go through before I started moving my shit through you. I guess that was the part that Will found hard to understand! It was all for the good baby, believe that!

"Hold up F!" Will held his hands up with this 'hold me back' gesture.

I was pissed the FUCK off! That shit right there, had me nervous as hell too!

Will continued, "Chill wit' all that, Ma! Let me finish handling what I'm doing then we can talk!"

"Naw nigga, we need to talk right now! Fuck all that!" I snapped with my arms folded over in a stanced position. I was pissed and he felt my wrath.

"Come on now…" He tried to convince me.

I pulled at his waist side. He just stared at me backing up over on the sidewalk.

"What the fuck?" He snapped,

"Listen! How you know this nigga?" I said as he gestured with this leveled hand motion moving it up and down as to tell me to lower my voice. Will would have *never* imagined I would have reacted like that but I was protecting my throne.

"Fauna, these yo peoples I thought?" He asked as if he only approved the deal because I knew the nigga.

I snapped back, "I know dude from school and the block but that's as far as it goes. This young swagless MF ain't cut for no shit like this baby!" I reassured him of my assessment of dude.

My voice carried across the neighborhood. I know I could be loud as hell, but fuck it. I was hot! Nosey muthafuckas on the block was staring hard like some shit was about to go down. Niggas love drama!

At that point I didn't give a fuck about who was listening. I was all about securing my shit!

"Hold up F. Listen to me for a minute."

I glanced over at Mason noticing me and Will talking, but he was trying to play it off like he was listening to some music, rocking his head from side to side. I knew better. His ass was all in. Sneaky ass devil faced mother fucker. I was boiling and irate at this point.

"Fauna... Fauna...!"

I was going in on his ass a mile a minute.

"Can I at least say this?" He begged.

"Say what," I snapped back.

I was becoming more agitated by the second!

"I thought homeboy was good peoples!"

Irritated as fuck I asked, "How you assume some shit like that? By him spittin' my name and saying we went to middle school together? That was enough for you to drop this kind of weight in his lap?" I took one step backwards giving him this confused ass look like *'Nigga fa'real! That's how we do around here?'*

Now I realized Will sometimes was a good judge of character, and I never really doubted that till then. Don't get me wrong now, I wanted to trust that all was well with the decision he made to fuck with this Wannabe-*Nino Brown* muthafucka, but I just couldn't fight the feeling I was having right then until he said,

"Fauna, dude copped 500 lbs from me two days ago and cashed me out *wit'* extras on the strength that I fronted him some of it!"

"Wait, you fronted him some of it...", I asked full of disbelief.

Before I could continue he cut me off.

"He had most of his bread up front and was very convincing that he was a man of his word and from the looks of it..."

He opened a duffle bag filled with cash he had just got from dude. I was impressed, but shit he better had came right. Something still didn't sit right with me. I don't know, it's just something about that paper that changes things in his favor. Maybe this *Mighty Mouse* lookin muthafucka may just be about that life. So there we were, fucking with a wanna-be-heartless-no backbone dope dealer from Southfield Michigan. I realized I was letting my guard down on the strength that my dude was validating this niggas position. Not to mention, he was spending that paper, so fuck it! I plucked the little green man off my shoulder and went on about my business, letting these two cats do their thang. The shit sounded good as hell to me at the time. Hell, it took exactly three niggas to do the kind of numbers Mighty Mouse did on the first go round so I found comfort in giving this nigga a chance by not listening to my first mind which later turned out to be another lesson learned. Damn...

17

"Wrong Place Wrong Time"

It was a little over a year when I started to notice some sloppiness with Mason. This was really starting to worry me, and I remember the day like it was yesterday! Roc was on the block when Mason pulled up. You know how it was when you see one of your peeps from the streets pull up in some nice shit talking bossy? You have this feeling of wanting to know how they are getting their money. Everybody from my hood wanted a chance to come up and Mason, from what he displayed to the block, looked like a nigga on the come up. I mean doing real good. So Roc, not thinking anything of it jumped his happy-go-lucky ass in the car and rolled with Mason on a run. He was cool with the crew so Roc felt like it was cool to role.

"What's up nigga!" Mason passed Roc the blunt as he slid into his passenger seat.

"I'm straight on that shit nigga!" Roc let out a small chuckle, sliding on his seatbelt.

"Bitch! HELL NAW! You gotta take that shit off dawg!" Mason pulled the blunt back toward his lips sucking in the excessive smoke from it into his lungs, and said, choking, "Nigga, you aint bout' to be riding up in my shit looking like Hermet-The-Playmate all strapped down and shit!" They laughed it off.

"Maaannn" Roc took the strap of the seatbelt that went across his chest and placed it under his arm to avoid it being as obvious.

"Look at you man!" Mason playfully hit him across his chest. "You all militant and shit! What the fuck happened to you?"

"You trippin dawg" Roc replied I'm that same nigga from the block. Just trying to build my chips, that's all."

"Is that right?" Mason asked blowing his horn at some big-booty chick walking into the liquor store as they rode past.

"Nigga you questioning me yet your ass still chasing pussy?" Roc teased.

"Chasing pussy!" Mason looked annoyed, feeling he had something to prove. He took his foot off the gas, and started pulling bands from under the seat as they sat at a traffic light on the corner of 6 mile and Wyoming. "Does this look like a nigga chasing pussy?!"

Roc's eyes got wide placing the circle of his hand over his mouth and said *"Daaaammmmn..."* he was amazed at the stacks he had.

"That's right bitch... *daammmnn*! I don't chase nothing but these fuckin dead presidents. This is what makes my dick hard nigga! Don't get me wrong playboy, I love me some pussy and I will step to it if it looks good from the outside. But, when it's time to grind, I'll snatch my dick out of a pretty bitch mouth, leaving her ass naked on her knees to go make that cash!" Mason said laughing loud as hell.

They continued to exchange stories back and forth as Mason headed over to his destination where he had a transaction set up and about to go down. This was not Roc's line of work. Roc was really laid back. He was one of those brainiac muthafuckas that could work out difficult shit. Things that don't make sense, Roc could unravel that shit in a matter of seconds and explain it to you like a muthafucka wit' a degree! He was cool to have around when a muthafucka was high and needed someone to think some shit through. He was the voice of reason when our brains were too cloudy. He was a leader in his own right; we respected him even more because he was loyal. He was just riding along taking in the excitement of hanging out with his balling-ass-friend this particular night, and not at all expecting things to change for the worse.

For some reason Roc jumped his ass in the car with Mighty Mouse, which kind of threw me off when I got the news, because Roc wasn't one of those follow-behind-a-nigga type. Not to mention, Mason came off as one of those bragging type niggas that the average thinker wouldn't risk going to a corner store with. This was why I knew from personal experience that Mason had to sound very convincing in order for Roc to even step foot into his car, and unknowingly ride to someone else's fate. That was so unlike Roc.

Night fell and those two were still bending corners in the city. It was the last stop before he dropped Roc back off to the spot. Mason had to meet this cat named Duke. I could clearly remember him saying dude's name when Will called him earlier that day. I be on some high shit, but my ass think clear as hell if the weed ain't no bullshit! He said Roc was with him and they were going to meet Duke. End of conversation. Anyhow, Duke was a longtime childhood friend as well whom I used to talk to back in my middle school days, some puppy love ass shit. Don't get it twisted tho'. A nigga had to put in work to fuck wit' this! I wasn't an easy chick to take off the market. Back to the story... unknowing to Mason, Duke who was also Mason's friend from middle school had made a plan with another nothing ass nigga to rob him. They premeditated their senseless plot to lay Mason the fuck down when he pulled up and exposed the work! However they expected Mason to arrive solo. They realized he had a passenger with him, but they didn't give a fuck. The plan had to be executed, them hoe ass niggas was hungry and the plan had to work out.

They pulled up to handle their transaction, and before Mason had a chance to see the two niggas exit the car with heaters blazin, it was too late. They walked vigorously towards the car riddling it with bullets. They hit Roc in the head and Mason in his neck and back! Duke and his fuck-boy pushed their bloodied bodies aside, snatched all the work and got the fuck on!! Blood was everywhere as Mason laid there clinging to life and it was over for Roc. It truly is cold in the D. But it's not just here, the entire fucking world is cold man. What was so fucked up was, Duke pumped the same nigga, who was once his childhood friend, full of lead over a punk ass 30lbs! Not even any other money, jewelry or any other shit they could go out and flip when the sun came up to get their money! They would have to take that bloody work to another muthafucka to cash them out. That's where the risk came in at. Somebody was gonna talk. Will and I were so deep in the streets we patiently waited for the streets to talk. As to be expected and like I told you before, word gets around really fast in the D. Not many muthafuckas were pulling the kind of weight me and my dude was. So whether Mason and Roc would have ended up dead or alive after that, nothing would have stopped us from getting to the bottom of that shit. You kill a nigga over some shit, you got to go back to the streets and sell it, and a nigga will get marked fast as hell for that shit!

It wasn't long before word got back to us what had happened. That's what was so gangsta about us we got the news before the news. We had our own street news team! When I caught wind of what had happened to Rocky Road, my nickname for Roc. I fell back in my seat. That nigga wasn't making a dime off that shit! He was just going along for the ride. This was why these anxious, trusting muthafuckas should fall back when going into situations on the strength of trust.

This was a dirty ass game and everybody ain't loyal. It's a not-give-a-fuck-about-you game! Ain't no loyalty in this shit! It's an every woman/man for him/herself game and it ain't worth the risk of being at the wrong place at the wrong time.

18

"My First Mind"

When I got word on the streets about what had happened with Mason and Roc I was fucked up! I don't know whether it was because I knew the muthafucka who set them up, or the fact that Roc died and Mason lived. It may sound harsh but I was feeling some kind of way! Two niggas alive and the only one dead is the main person that didn't deserve it. Although I hate hospitals I needed answers so I was on my way.

When I got up to the hospital - the smell of death lingered in the air and it was overwhelming. I proceeded to room 1124 which was where Mason was. I still remember seeing him attached to all of these tubes and IV's, trying to recover from his near-death experience. I was trying to get straight to the point being that I didn't have any information as to who, what and where all of this went down. I knew he was recovering but I didn't give a fuck how much morphine he was on. He was gonna tell me what I needed to know because I was ready for some gangsta shit! Let's be clear. I wasn't there to visit this muthafucka on some sympathy shit! I wanted to know who the fuck took my dope so I could handle mines.

I had seen the two detectives exit his hospital room as I made my way down the hall. I became even more furious because I knew he was a hoe ass nigga to the core.

"What's up Mason? How you holding up?" I said softly sliding into his room and standing on the side of his bed while the nurse was taking his vitals on the other side.

He struggled to turn his neck in my direction. I could tell he was in some serious pain.

"Hey F." He struggled in a raspy tone.

My presence seemed to put a little hostility in the air. Maybe my facial expressions gave it away, or maybe it was my tone. His blood pressure began to rise. She checked the monitor then glanced at me. I gave her ass a look and she began to move a little faster, removing some bloody bandages from the table and walking over toward the door, but I knew she was not gone. I could tell she started dragging her feet, and I noticed her stalling looking down at something on a clipboard. I personally thought she was trying to ear hustle from afar.

"Excuse me…" I approached her nosey ass.

She looked up from the clipboard with a fake smirk. She was this young black chick that I could tell had this curious look on her face as to who I was.

"Yes." She responded in this lazy-uninterested-in-what-the-fuck I wanted tone.

"Yes, if you don't mind, if you're done with him, I need to have a word with my brother."

She looked at me like *'and… you say this to say what?'* Yet only responded with an, "Oh ok… no problem." She swayed her wide hips out the door and I pushed it up behind her ass.

Mason stared up at the TV as if he was lost in thought. "So, what happened dawg? Was it Duke?" I asked I knew he had been questioned already because when I was walking in, the detectives were walking out! At first it appeared as if he was ignoring me.

I instantly asked, "You ain't talk to them did you!?" I pointed my finger in a gesturing motion in the direction of the door.

To my surprise he answered,

"*Uhhhrrr.*" He made a painful grunting noise that I assumed came from his stomach and side where he had been stitched up from the bullet wounds. The nigga was fucked up for real! Matter of fact, just looking at his ass had me hurting all over! He continued, "Yeah F, you know they already knew what happened!"

WOWWWW! I rolled my eyes out of frustration.

"That nigga Duke didn't get the $100,000 that was under my seat F, but the detectives did Ma, along with a few bows I had in the trunk!" he said releasing a painful cough.

I was speechless. I couldn't utter another word to this dumb ass nigga that I *knew would fold* if he was ever confronted in a tight situation.

"Maaannn…you just admitted that you told… You know that was supposed to be taken to the streets right." I said calmly at first and then I lost it, thinking how dumb this nigga could have been to tell the fucking detectives that shit knowing how we roll!

"Mason! Are You Fuck'n Serious Dawg! He killed our manz!!"

UUHHHGGGH! I just quietly exited the room fool of rage. Before I could even make it to the elevator Mason was cut the fuck off!! I kept him close tho, always been rules and levels to this game. I would give him enough money to pay off a few bills and feed me more bullshit. I told Will this nigga was not cut for the streets! I have been knowing this nigga. Now his ass was hot and couldn't hustle for us anymore. He would keep asking us for work and one day the little nigga inside of me decided I had to one day tell dude,

"Yo Mason check this out, you told the police dawg... THE POLEEECE", I uttered as if I was retarded.

He must have been a retard to fuckin talk to the police any damn way. I further explained to him, although I didn't have to, you told the police what went down before you told us "....and you think Imma put my shit in your hands again? So let me be as blunt as this muthafucka I'm smoking on hanging from my lips right now... YOU WILL NEVAH HUSTLE WITH ME AGAIN! And if you want to maintain what's left of what we have now, I would strongly advise you to stop asking me. So let's do you and me a favor and roll with the two'z and few'z I'm giving you to help yo ass get by. Believe me Mason, many would say I'm being nice, because personally, I didn't want to give you shit after what happened, but I prayed on it and this is where we stand! Furthermore, I ain't that fucked up out here!" I said to him looking serious as hell.

He just stared at me in awe. I didn't give a fuck. I was on a role. I just kept kicking his dumb ass while he was down. I fuckin hate snitches!

I continued, "So as of now, I would encourage you to either get a job or find a new hustle baby. That's the best I can offer you at this time, and that advice didn't cost yo' ass a dime!"

I pulled smoke from my blunt and blew it in the opposite direction of where he sat, and then passed it to his lame ass frontin' like shit was cool. Hell, in my mind it was. I guess he didn't take what I said too kindly. He had this look in his eyes that read *'What dis bitch jus say to me! Fuck is shu'!'* but hell, he was a snitch ass nigga and I wasn't giving his ass an opportunity to get me caught up on some of his bullshit!

Shortly after that conversation, it wasn't long before he jumped in the bed with another one of Will's manz we called D. By then I had grown tired of schooling niggas on what was up out here with these unseasoned ass wanna be street niggas in the game. I had come to the realization that I had to protect mines by all means necessary in the end, because when it came to a woman out here getting money; muthafuckas looked at us from an entirely different perspective. They don't take us seriously until they get fucked up.

I thought D, on the other hand, could read niggas and see their dog shit before steppin in it. At least that was the D I thought I knew. I met Diddy when I met Will back when I was 19. Diddy reminded me so much of the rapper Jay Z, he had the big lips and everything, and this was Wills manz! They were more like brothers, they were inseparable. When Will touched ground and we got back together Diddy started coming back around like clockwork. He wasn't doing well financially, but he had good direction and ideas, and I respected that. He just needed a little boost to bounce back, and I was willing to make it happen for him - dude was cool people.

At the time I was doing very well. I had this attitude that if I was rocking some sweet shit, everyone in my circle would have the same. That was the kind of bitch I was. I loved to shine, but not outshine the ones I called family and friends.

Furthermore, I learned firsthand, it eliminates a lot of jealousy which me and my circle did not need. So, since I was out on shopping sprees buyin up Rolexes and yellow diamonds and shit I made sure Diddy's wrist was graced with one of Rolex's best. With that came some work. I wanted him to feel like he was a part of something wholesome. So I fronted him more than enough to pay me back and show himself some love. As time went on, and my stash got fatter, business was doing swell. Diddy was in Will's ear about them getting their own connects.

Although I felt some kind of way at first, I was seasoned enough in the game to know how hard it was for men to accept female hustlers getting money like I was. I ran my own empire and had my own ends. I was a hustlers dream and he couldn't come to grips with that. So when he greeted me with a smile, I smiled back. I knew what was behind it all, but I didn't want to lose sight of what was, so I played the part. I was mature enough to realize that sometimes you must follow before you can lead. Study, learn, and listen are some of the strengths that made me the successful woman I was then and am now.

Will sunk so much work and money into Diddy to a point where I was noticing shit wasn't really comin back in return, and I was frustrated with that shit. We were in this to make money not lose money, but there came a time when you have to call a spade a spade and this muthafucka was not dealing from the right deck! The only thing I was noticing was new clothes, new cars and bitches galore! I would ask Will what the nigga was on? Because there was constant work and money going out but hardly nothing coming in, and homeboy or not, muthafucka this was business and I needed some answers.

Will would always tell me he had everything under control but hell, I couldn't tell! So when I caught wind that Mason and Diddy were now bosom buddies, something came over me like a horrible cold without a cure. That was a feeling that forced me to keep my third eye open. It was just a matter of time before the wolves in sheep's clothing would reveal themselves. I just hoped it wouldn't have been under my watch because I was taking no prisoners. Everybody was gonna feel my wrath if I was betrayed, and I wasn't the kind of bitch a nigga wanted to back into a corner.

19

"Tales From The Hood"

"My name is Reekah bitch!", yelled the owner of Salon Crazee Cutz & Stylez .

She was screaming at some fat ass chick while some of the stylists and onlookers held them both back from beating the shit out of each other. After the fat chick had just ran up in Reekah's salon off 8mile and Southfield, and snuck her ass from behind. These hoes were clowning! I slid past the chaos. For me it was just another crazy day in the D. I was just trying to get my damn nails and toes done, my same routine every other week unless I broke one or two in between. But, like always Reekah and her drama always made my visits something to look forward to! It was like havin a front row seat at the season finale of a reality show.

The irate fat female screamed over the people who were holding her back throwing her finger up in the air,

"HOE IMMA KILL YOU IF YOU KEEP FUCKING WIT' MY MAN!", trying to fight her way through them to get to Reekah.

It was not happening tho.

"Well I'm ready to die bitch!" Reekah snapped back with her arms open wide in a *'here I am bitch, bring it'* motion as they pushed the angry fat chick out the door. Reekah just calmly swayed her wide hips over to her client that was waiting franticly at her workstation. To her it was nothing, she continued on like nothing happened.

"It's always something jumping off in here. Yall bitches are crazy!" I said laughing out loud.

"Why you think I named this bitch Crazee Cutz?" Reekah taunted.

"Why cause yo' *crazee* ass will *cut'a* bitch?!" The he-she intervened standing in front of a mirror fixing his lipgloss and popping his damn lips.

Now the he-she was another story in itself! Last week Dereon, the he-she, who happened to occupy the station next to Reekah, had a falling out with one of the other stylists, Tawanda, after confronting her about her in-the-closet husband coming onto him one day when Tawanda was running behind for her client. I guess Tawanda's dude had popped up supposedly looking for her and some words were exchanged between him and Dereon. Ironically, the salon was empty. Everyone, was gone leaving them two there alone this particular day. One thing lead to another and shit got real up in that bitch!!

Dereon pulled Tawanda to the side to avoid embarrassing her arrogant ass in front of everyone, and told her what had happened and she went off calling him a Drag Queen and all kinds of demeaning and derogatory shit! Tawanda did not want to believe her dude loved dick more than he loved her - I guess I couldn't blame her. I honestly couldn't fathom the thought myself.

That was what weekly visits at the salon usually consisted of. One minute a bitch could be sewing in a weave while the next minute somebody could be snatching yo' shit out and not professionally neither! Dem' hoes went for blood over at Cutz. Whoop ass first, then ask questions later. That was the jump off spot fareal!

I was good with all their crazy asses, even Dereon which was one of my faves. Though Dereon was one of the hottest in the game when it came to short and sassy looks, he was also well known for hiding large sums of packaged dope in his ass when moving weight for niggas. I guess gay niggas could be useful after all. Think of it - what male officer do you know would subject himself into checking up in a flame thrower's asshole for some dope if it came down to it! The testosterone in men would not allow them to actually do something like that which worked in their favor. Reekah got her shit under control and we all smoked a few blunts and shared a few laughs about the fat chick's dude that her slutty ass was fuckin on the side.

"Reekah, you're one of the baddest side-bitches I ever known." Dereon teased in his feminist tone.

"And you know this…" She responded in confidence passing the blunt back to me.

"Girl you gon' fuck around and one of these tack heads gon' catch yo' ass slippin'! Like she just did!" Dereon laughed.

The fat chick did slice a nice one in on her. She was wearing the shit out of that scar tho'.

"Fauna, I aint worried about these insecure hoes out here trying to compete with my pretty ass fareal!" Going back to styling her client's hair, she said, "Yeah dat bitch got one up on me. All is well. I Got something for her ass tho'! That stunt she just pulled running up in my shit on me like that will be dealt wit'!"

Reekah was a well-known hoe in the D that fucked with damn near every nigga I knew that was in the streets.

She definitely had her share. But to each his own was how I saw it. I was too caught up in my own problems and drama to be focused on a bitch that competed with who-can-suck-the-largest-dick-with-the-most-lesions that swore she was top-of-the-line out here in these streets. Bitch couldn't hide them big ass herpes sores around her lips with the most expensive Mac lipstick, but that hoe was getn' it in, gracing the cover of The Cason's Hair Magazine and getting the #1 Hairstyle Award every year and I wasn't mad at her.

Miles were flipped over on that pussy, turned back a few times and stopped rolling multiple times from so many niggas running up in that shit. But to still be fighting over some dick, 'Bitch, Get'cho life!' I can't lie now, she was one of the coldest hairstylists in the game, and her side chick named Glamour, who did my nails, was the icing on the cake for her business. I had so much crazy shit going on in my head that day, a muthafucka could have threw a chair at my ass knocking me over my head and I woulda gave a love-live-life pass. So while being surrounded by a fucking shrine circus and forced to have to listen to these clowns, I was still trying to swallow the pill from the "Diddy and Mason" interception. Out the blue these niggas had started hanging tight shortly after Roc got killed, and his bitch ass told the police Duke shot him!!

Word up at Crazee Cutz was these niggas was down in Miami renting whole floors at the Loews Hotel, and buying out the bar at Club Mansion on some P-Diddy shit! I couldn't believe it!! This was the same nigga that just told Will that our $750,000 was just gone because the load got hit! He went on to saying how he was fucked up and was waiting on the Mexicans to front him something to cover the loss he had with us. The same nigga that asked for another $500,000 and swore on his life that 500 would get everything back poppin and on track!!

The million dollar question me and Will had was, why this hoe ass nigga would be out in Miami spending a half a million in one night with an outstanding debt with us?! Shit wasn't adding up, and I knew damn well this nigga didn't think he was dealing with a fool! I am a pretty bitch, but I am far from dumb. I may be deeply in love but I still had my eyes on my throne. Did he really think Will and I was just gonna lay back and let him slide while he was just blowing our money like that!!

Just when we thought shit was fucked up, this fool owed the connect 10 million! So that bullshit about coming up after he bumped into them was some straight BS because they weren't givin' him shit! See, D was used to livin a certain lifestyle so he was using *our* money that Will's dumb ass kept giving to him, to keep his fucked up spending and trickin habits on track!! Ain't that some shit?! The money we grinded for, risked our lives for, and would kill for, was being used to help another nigga shine for some nothin ass niggas and some dust bucket hoes. Hard to believe, but picture this - these two cats, who at one time would become some of our worst enemies, would also one day hold the key to our freedom sooner than we could have ever anticipated.

20

"Too Close For Comfort"

I've realized over time and through my own personal experiences that all people go through different obstacles in their lives. Sometimes the bad outweighs the good, somebody dies, a baby is born, life is always constantly going on. As seconds turn into minutes, minutes turn into hours, hours turn into days, days turn into months and months turn into years. The time will pass and you never want to regret not using it wisely. They say you should always take advantage of the time you have on this earth, seems cliché I know, but honestly why do we not take advantage of our time?

There I was, lost in deep thought about all the shit going on around me and my family, when out the blue, before we could even address one situation, there came another, only this time it was way too close to home! It was at that very moment I felt it wasn't going to be long before I would have to come face to face with my demons, there was just so much evilness going on right next door! It wouldn't be long before fate came to pay me another visit. The phone rang, and I don't know why, but I felt this sense of nervousness or paranoia when I answered it, but I answered anyway.

"Hello?" I answered, apprehensively.

"F, SOME NIGGAS JUST TRIED TO ROB MY MOMS!"

"WHAT?!" I yelled through the phone tripping over my tongue trying to get my words to fall in line, because shit I was in shock!

Before I hung up I had already transformed from my g-string, to fully dressed, and running out of the crib like a bolt of lightning. The only thing racing through my mind at that time was *'whoever the fuck did this shit couldn't possibly know how we got down out here in these streets! They had to be some fucking amateurs!'*

Once I got on the block and met up with the family, I learned that somebody had forced their way into Momma Fran's house at gunpoint demanding money! What the fuck?! The Mom's?! Fa'real tho'?! Will's mom was cool as hell too! She was the type of mom you can kick it wit' about damn near anything. Honestly, she should have been a comedian in her day, because she was funny as fuck. Momma Fran would be cracking jokes and frying chicken. She was naturally funny, always kicking some real OG shit. Some of the things she would say would be alluring, and I would try to remember those little phrases to use for my t-shirt line. I loved and respected her for accepting me for who I was.

She never judged me or treated me like I was just one of Will's bitches, like most Moms who have issues with their son's girlfriends. I was more like the daughter she never had. I could be down or under the weather, and when she walked into the room she changed the atmosphere into something warm and positive. I loved her, our connection was deep and the mere thought of someone fucking with her had me feeling some kind of way.

139

Something had to be done, and I wasn't going to sleep until we got to the bottom of who was behind this.

After meeting with the family, I met up with Will in the streets and we raced up the Lodge Freeway, headed to Momma Fran's. No radio, no talking. You could hear the wind as we zipped past the cars. Will was driving whipping in and out of traffic. Both of our minds racing even faster than the car, trying to figure out who was crazy enough to do some shit like this. Only trustworthy family and friends were allowed around Momma Fran. We exit off the freeway barely pausing for the light. We pulled up in front of Momma Fran's like a muthafucka in a high speed chase, Will damn near broke the handle on the door trying to get to her, and my ass was on his heels breaking two nails and snagging my $1,200 *Ferragamo* blouse.

The house was so huge it took what seemed like forever to make it to the front door from sprinting across the front lawn. My ass was out of breath too! Hell, I smoked too much damn weed to be running and shit! Momma Fran was going crazy and crying hysterically. We could barely make out what she was trying to say. Just watching her break down fucked me up. The fear in her eyes, the tremble in her voice was so familiar to me. She thanked God, she praised God she was happy to be alive. I knew how she felt all too well. Will on the other hand had the devil in his eyes. To see his Mom in distress was a terrible feeling! I knew this was just the beginning.

"I WANT TO KNOW WHO THE FUCK DID THIS?" Will snapped walking off mad as fuck!

Will had this way of dealing with his emotions privately, but I could see and feel his anger and frustration as much as he tried to hide it from me. I know my babe; I knew what he was thinking. I know what he was feeling. Being on the bad side of what the good life has to offer is never an easy pill to swallow. But they disrespected his Mother. Things have most definitely escalated to the highest level. Some of the other family members were embracing Momma Fran, which gave me a small window of opportunity to find Will.

"Babe!" I said, walking in on him on his phone.

He held his finger up gesturing me to hold on. I already knew where the conversation was going. Muthafuckas better know. Shit was about to get real!

"F, I think I know who did this..." He pondered hanging up his phone.

"I bet it was that dirty ass nigga on the block baby!" I said as I lit a blunt to try and calm the atmosphere.

"Brilliant minds think alike." He said, as he pulled smoke from the blunt.

Before he could pass it back we were off and running on some Bonnie and Clyde shit. Our lives were like a tornado. You never knew who or what would get caught up in our storm. These desperate fools had the balls to knock on Momma Fran's door and as soon as she answered it they pushed their way inside! It was obvious they had come with a vengeance. They hit her nephew Dante across the head with the gun, and tied them up! It was blatantly obvious what they wanted, money! The crazy part of this was there was no money hid up in her shit! Why would these muthafuckas think that anyway I thought to myself?!! She was mortified. We learned after that they snatched up $9,000 she had saved in a shoebox, her fur coats, TVs, Play Station and some other elementary shit.

Leading us to believe, it had to have been some young wannabe gangstas!!

Momma Fran kept asking herself who would do this to her, being that she was such a free hearted soul and would give anyone the shirt off her back. But me and Will had a hunch who these masked bitch-ass niggas were. My feelings were hurt that I could only make assumptions, but I based shit off facts because when I come for that ass, there won't be any mistaken identities on that hit list.

21

"From Worse to Worst"

When it rains it pours...Just when Will and I had to face the traumatic situation with his Mom being robbed, then came the BOOM! Drama with his baby mama...

Shaunie Davis was the mother of Will's daughter Alexis who we called Lex. Though Will and Shaunie had their ups and downs, me or Will never wished bad on her. We absolutely never wanted something this crazy to happen to her. Beyond the bullshit, a child that we all loved was involved. When we got the news of what happened to Shaunie, I was sure it would affect Lex for the rest of her life, she witnessed the whole thing. Another life gone, another motherless daughter. Just another day in the city of Detroit. Unfortunately, her future had absolutely no promise in this cold world we live in.

Lex and I became even closer. I was like a second Mom to her. She opened up to me about anything she couldn't talk to her Mom about, which I thought was really cool. We had this bond, this connection that I wanted to have with my own child one day. But after what happened, it seemed like she had been pushed into this shell. I honestly felt at that very moment that I had not only lost the trusting nature of my stepchild, it was almost like losing my best friend. Every time she would close me out I would give her all the space she needed in the hope that one day she'd allow me back in. I never saw myself giving up on her no matter what. I was going to allow her time to come around, and it wasn't long before she found her way into my arms to release a world of pain and tragedy that no child should have to bear.

One day after having this psychological episode with Lex I knew something had to give. Surprisingly, after some reassurance and moral support, she opened up, and what she told me will haunt my soul for the rest of my life. What happened to her Mom that night changed all of our lives. As she lay on her bed with her back turned to me and balled up in the fetal position, I played in her hair telling her how she never really wanted anyone to comb her hair but me. When she let out this friendly snicker only moments after her blow up, I knew she was coming around.

I was in the dark about what happened that night with Shaunie. Lex was the only one that saw exactly what happened to her Mom at only thirteen years old; and almost a year later all of the layers of that tough skin she hid behind had suffocated her, forcing her to face the reality of her situation. I sat there in awe listening to this heart-wrenching story that had me a little apprehensive. I could clearly see how it affected her. Lex went on to describe the scene of events that led up to the murder of her Mom that had taken place. She said the last time she saw her Mom alive and well was when she went upstairs into her room to ask her if she could go get them something to eat. She mentioned that Shaunie had slept the whole day prior to her waking her up. Shaunie hadn't realized at the time that she had slept so long and she jumped up out the bed out of her deep sleep coma. She rubbed her eyes not realizing how much time had passed by.

Lex sat at the foot of her Mom's bed resting her chin against the palm of her open hand that rested on her knee. The only thing she could remember was watching her Mom go from room to room appearing to be rushing off somewhere. Shaunie sighed as she stood at her bathroom sink that was adjacent to the bed where Lex sat watching her every move. She admired her Mom by always being observant. Shaunie loved her daughter. Lex was truly her little ball of sunshine and they were very close.

Throwing water against her face and trying to shake off that urge to jump back in bed, Shaunie glanced over at Lex and winked. Moments after that intimate bat from Shaunie's eye, Lex heard her phone ring and she answered, hearing the voice of her Dad Will and Grandma Fran on the three-way. Lex went on to inquire about a dog tag her dad had just bought for her.

They shared a very intense conversation about how he was going to spend more time with her. Even Grandma Fran talked about how much she wanted the family to be more close-knit. The conversation went on for a little over an hour. "WOW! I was on the phone that long?" She stared at the headset, placing it on the nightstand. It had gotten late and she hadn't noticed Shaunie had slid out on her hours prior. All she knew was that they were waiting on some Coney Island that never came. By then, live-in cousin Kajuan and Lex had given up on their chili cheese fries, cheese sticks and Coney dog with all the extras, and made their way into the room where they shared a bunk bed. Lex got on the bottom bunk while Kajuan climbed on top.

Like every night before falling asleep, Lex would carry on a conversation with Kajuan until one of them gave in and fell asleep. This particular night Kajuan was the first to go down for the count. It wasn't long after that when she heard what sounded like a car pulling up. Lex climbed out her bed to peak through her window to check and see if it was her Mom. It was in fact her Mom pulling into her parking space in the rental truck she was driving at the time. To her surprise Lex could see off in the darkness what appeared to be three people dressed in black popping up out the bushes!

That's when everything went ballistic! Lex looked on in horror. Her Mom got out her truck, and three masked assailants approached her with guns, catching her off guard! The look on her Mom's face would be forever engraved in Lex's mind. It was the last time she saw her Mother alive! Lex's heart started to race! It was like she was caught in the middle of a horror film! She banged against the window in an attempt to alert her Mom about the people wearing the masks, but it was too late, they quickly pulled out their guns. They stood in a lit up area by the parking spot with the light beaming on Shaunie. Before she could utter a scream or a cry for help, the three masked people raised their weapons and opened fire. Shaunie's lifeless body fell to the ground. After being shot multiple times, it was obvious she never stood a chance of surviving. Lex's loud screams combined with the bullets that riddled through the darkness outside her bedroom window were piercing.

Kajuan jumped up out of his sleep to Lex yelling, "THEY KILLING MY MAMA! THEY KILLING MY MAMA!"

Kajuan went into a rage and tried to run down the steps. Lex was so afraid for both of them, and with impulse tackled him down before he was able to get to the door! Lex remembered clearly begging her cousin not to go out that door, smart thinking for a kid who knew if these people were bold enough to kill her Mom, they would have no issues killing them, no witnesses. Lex's mind went blank! She couldn't even remember the number to 911 as she sat in a cradled position on the floor with the phone in her hand rocking back and forth, crying profusely. This baby was in the middle of a living nightmare. I knew it was hard for her to relive this tragic night, but I'm glad she felt comfortable enough to talk to me about it. Lex going into detail about her Mom's death will always, and I mean always, be etched in the back of my mind. I can still remember that night as if it had just happened. I couldn't believe what she had come face to face with. It was like a massacre!

Will and I rushed to the scene as soon as we got the call. We were forced to have to sit through, and watch the aftermath of everything that transpired. Pulling up to the murder scene, I used my hand to block the view of her body laying under a sheet on the cold ground in my peripheral. I was nervous as hell and very uncomfortable but I knew I had to be strong for the kids though. I just had to. As the police roped off the crime scene and her body laid on the ground for what seemed like hours, I held Lex as tight as I could, not wanting to ever let her go. From that day forward, I became her shield. I have this notion that I need to protect her from the fucked up shit in the world she'll one day have to go through. I knew from this day forward I wanted to always be there for her if she really needed me, no matter what, I wasn't goin NOWHERE!

Will and I knew what we had to do as parents. We accepted the challenge, stepped up and took full responsibility for Alexis. We didn't hesitate in picking up the pieces from where Shaunie had left off. I embraced her like I birthed her myself, often mindful of the fact that I knew nothing could replace the love of her Mom. I just wanted to be that one she could turn to and be there for her in times of need. I knew there would be a rough road ahead and I was determined to help her get through it. That was truly my only intention, and as time went on our relationship grew closer, but her wounds were just bandaged and never had time to heal.

Paranoia meant certain behaviors remained, such as not being able to sleep in a room by herself, and a lack of conversation when in a room filled with family. We began to consider the question of seeking therapy for her. I think what gave me that push was when I went looking for her in our home one day, and she was nowhere to be found until something told me to check under her bed. She was sleeping like a bear in hibernation. Scared the shit out of me! That wasn't it though! She had this thing that no matter how hot it may have been in the house she would snuggle up in the closet with tons of blankets! That was when I told Will the whole counseling and therapy idea was something we may want to consider as soon as possible. It was blatantly obvious that Lex was still terrified. I felt hopeless, that I couldn't help her, so to me getting her some professional help was the next best thing.

Outside of Will and I, Lex spent all her time alone. She became so isolated in her own little world; she shared very little emotions toward things your average youth her age would care about. She was numb on the inside and her eyes proved it. She went from having some emotions, to being emotionless. She became very cold hearted and that troubled me. Though her cold callousness was something I had to keep a 3rd eye on, she was very observant of her surroundings through it all. Lex became our eyes and ears. She made sure she watched and listened to everything around her. Some may call this ear hustling, while others may look at it as her being way too involved in grown folks business. Many said I spoiled her, but I ignored they ass. Lex got the world from me, and I'm pretty sure if they were in my shoes taking on a responsibility of the child of their significant other, they too would have done the same thing. So, middle finger to anyone challenging me and mines. Lex was our bulldog in the family. She could sometimes come off as not giving a fuck. It was a reflection of all she had endured.

It was always family first and bullshit last with her and that was the glue that held us all together. We all had our moments and there were times when Lex may have not agreed with some of my rules, but at the end of the day, Fauna knew best!

22...

"Anger was one Letter Short of Danger"
-Dr. Robert Anthony

All of the crazy shit that had happened over a period of two months was a lot to take in. Will was livid and I was stressin'! At one point I thought he was going to lose it and go on a killing spree! His Moms! His baby girl! AWW HELL NAW! This nigga became a monster overnight! The truth of the matter was, we couldn't just hit the streets of Detroit and start killing everybody we *thought* had something to do with that robbery situation at Momma Fran's. Shit was just getting out of control and it was hitting too close to home.

Throughout all the drama in the streets, Lex moving in with us, helping her through her pain and my ass ended up pregnant. This was way too much to bare. You should have seen my ass; I was all over the place mentally, emotionally, physically.

"Tia! Bitch where you at?!" I said frantically on the other end of the phone.

"Gettin' some dick bitch...mmmh..." she moaned.

"Eeeeeew HOE! What the fuck you answer the phone for! That shit is gross!" I giggled.

Tia ass was crazy as hell. I couldn't help but to laugh at that shit. In spite of the fact that I was feeling messed up at that very moment and in dire need to talk to a friend, that bitch pulled me out of my depression wit' that crazy shit. I swear she was the only one of my friends that would answer her phone in the middle of getting some head or riding some dick. That's the real Lil Kim while they playin'. I hung up and called my other girl.

Thankfully Robin answered the phone. I needed someone to talk to right then, I couldn't wait a minute longer! I was pacing back and forth damn near burning a hole in my expensive ass carpet. I had a pregnancy stick in my hand shaking that bitch constantly. I was praying to Allah, God, Buddha who ever in the hell would listen that the plus sign I was seeing through the small window of plastic was just a defect. I honestly thought it wasn't possible after I had ran through one box of pregnancy test and purchased damn near three other different brands but I was still hopeful. I just knew my ass would get a different answer other than positive! It took me a minute to realize of course this would have happened to me at such a time like this.

"Oh shit shit shit," I said as my mind was totally confused.

"Gurrl... You may as well relax and face that shit. You knocked up bitch and that's all, it is not the end of the world." My so-called friend teased.

"This is not a joking matter bitch. I got so much shit to do right now and having a baby was not in the plan." I said

"So what you gonna name her?" She asked as if the sex of the few weeks old fetus had been determined.

She ignored my frantic behavior, kept blowing bubbles and smacking on some gum through the phone irritating my last nerve. That shit went straight through me;

151

I hung up on her ass. I was still at a loss for words, shaking my head, walking over to the mirror in the bathroom and saying, "This has got to be a sign..."

I pondered and pondered about what I was gonna do. *Me being a Mom??* I didn't know much about having no kids at that time. I was about my bread! How the hell does a Mother and a hustler become one? Mother in the day, hustler at night? Wait then who would read the baby the traditional bed time stories like my Mom did when I was young? If I was going to become a Mother I wanted to be the best Mom I could be. I just was not sure how I was going to make that happen and continue to live as I have. But, like I said before, Lex really made this puzzle of madness complete for me. Once I came to terms that I was officially pregnant and the more I started to show, it seemed to make Lex happy. Her anticipation was like waiting on a gift from Santa. She would smile as she asked a million questions.

"What are you going to name the baby? Do you know what you're having yet? Is she going to look like me and my Dad?" She asked so many questions but I didn't mind.

I was glad she was happy about something, looking forward to the baby and just her being involved was good for the both of us. *Wow, really Lex?* I thought to myself trying to imagine which face I wanted my baby to wear for the rest of her life. Would the baby look like me and my side of the family or her Dad's? Lex went on with the 21 questions, and damn near drove me nutz. I had to admit to the fact that I hadn't seen her that excited since before her Mom was killed and seeing how excited she was really touched my heart.

"Will she have your pretty hair, Fauna? How long does it take for a baby to start walking? Will I be able to babysit? Will you love us both the same?" Lex rattled on and on with the questions and I just listened to her nodding my head yes and no, I don't know, and I knew what her calling was - lawyer!

All dem' damn questions in one breath! The child never once exhaled! She was going straight to law school and she didn't even know it.

Once I broke the news about my new beginning to Will and our families they were just as happy and anticipating my new arrival as Lex and I was. Before my 3rd trimester I was eating up and spitting up and still blowing up! It didn't take long before it had really sunk in that ya girl was really having a baby.

23

"The Baby Shower"

Here I was reflecting on the life I had unwittingly chosen – *Robberies, killings, AND A CHEATING ASS HUSBAND*!!

One might ask, "Bitch, how do you handle all of this shit by yourself?" And I would just respond, "I'm a boss and boss bitches like me are born with tough skin and already planned futures."

I knew since I was barely out of diapers I would be rich. I had a burning sensation in my belly that always wanted more than anyone could give me. That feeling went away when I started to see the fruits of my beautiful hustle. I loved, lived and dominated board games like *Monopoly* and *Chess* as early as age 5 so as I sat back and reminisced on this life of becoming a Mom/Step-Mom/wife/daughter-in-law and certified hustler. I knew I was going to make the best out of a mess; I was good at making the best out of the worst. It was one of my gifts.

Throughout my pregnancy, I wanted to do the same shit I had been doing before I found out I was pregnant. You know, that once-in-a-lifetime shit. That was why planning a baby shower was huge to me! Will was on some fuck-boy shit, which was common for some men when they get their bitches pregnant. They wanna fuck around with side-bitches and run the fucking streets all damn night!

So, being that I didn't have a big dream girl wedding by us eloping. I planned an unforgettable baby shower that was every boss bitch's fantasy! Hell, I still wanted my wedding though. I woulda been planning that shit then if it wasn't for Mister-Buss-A-Nut all up in my shit, knocking a bitch up right after we eloped. So the gigantic wedding I was planning to take place on our first year anniversary was put on hold because I was not about to walk down anybody's aisle big and pregnant as hell! I decided to put all my creative thoughts and thousands of dollars into the baby shower for our baby girl.

You talking about one of the most beautiful baby showers anyone had ever seen. At least 350 people came. $10,000 was spent on pink roses, $20,000 for Dom-P and Moet fountains, a chocolate fountain for the strawberries and other fruits on our elaborate display of crab legs, fried lobster, the works! We even had massage tables set up! This lavish event was going to be the talk of the town, but really should have been on Entertainment TV.

There was a room in the basement we set up for the men with a bunch of flat screens with Play Stations and X-Boxes with every fucking game you could think of! OH! And I can't forget the strippers! I had that shit set up like a muthafuckn' bachelor party fo' they ass! It was some shit nobody that attended had ever seen before!! We ended up spending about $50,000 total on the baby shower. Some may have called this crazy spending or even a little over-the-top. But me, I called it a once in a lifetime thing. I swear I got so many gifts that I didn't have to buy our baby a damn thing for a few years - literally!! I even gave stuff away because I had damn near 2 or 3 of everything. Nice shit too!

I had so much shit I needed a U-Haul to take my gifts home! Just to name a few of the nice gifts I received - I'm talking 20 pairs of Gucci's, no bullshit! There were 10 Christian Dior outfits and muthafucka's Dolce and Gabbana'd me to death!! She had all kinds of sets of jewelry just like her Mommy and Daddy, diamonds for the princess!! I mean, my baby got anything and everything one child could imagine and she hadn't even gotten here yet! My jeweler Gary, from Golden Suns, and his Mom even came! *So, don't be fooled by the rocks that we got...*! They presented an unforgettable gift for our baby that still to this very day I have locked in my safety deposit box. It was this gorgeous diamond heart pendant! So-so beautiful!

After this day I thought me and Will may have had a chance to make it forever. I put aside his recent hoe-ish activities and enjoyed one of my most memorable moments with our closest friends and family. What a fool I was to even halfway believe this nigga would change! He was the same asshole he was before we had separated, and I would take him back over and over again. Like the song said, *everybody plays the fool...* and I was a fool in love and my pregnant emotions had my mind, heart and soul in disagreement with my decision to stay.

24

"The One Who Loves the Least Controls the Relationship"
-Dr. Robert Anthony

After our little bundle of joy was born, Will couldn't wait to come up with a name for our daughter. When he came up with Bobbi Joe I thought the nigga was high off some shit. I didn't hesitate coming up with a name of my own which he loved – Fanesse. And that was the name we gave our daughter. It was soft, with an edge.

Fanesse changed the game when she got here. And thank god for Lex being there to help me with her little sis! I honestly couldn't tell you what life would have been like without her. Will was caught up in the streets with the business and hoes while I sat at home playing the stay-at-home Mom and Wife. Fuck all that! I was not cut from that cloth. It was bad enough both of them reminded me of him so much, I had to pull some strength out of somewhere and shake this nigga's hold off of me! I had just had our daughter and now it was time for me to get back to doing me. I had to. He wasn't about the life that I was giving a hundred and one percent to at that time. It was all about the kill for him. All that trying to live with him didn't do anything for my mental state. It actually fucked my head up even more. Every day it was some new chick, and a new lie he was telling. The more I learned the truth about his hoeish ways, the more I wanted out of the relationship, but, walking away would have been really hard for me, being that I was all in. My parents had been together forever, getting married, staying married and raising our children as my parents had was my ultimate goal. He clearly had a different plan.

Dr. Robert Anthony, a well known author, had a popular book called *Think Big*. In it there was a quote I remember that read, *"The One Who Loves The Least Controls The Relationship"*. I obviously didn't allow those words to marinate long in my system, or maybe this nigga somehow read the quote before my ass did!

I can think back, even before I had Fanesse how dude started having affairs and shit! In fact, I don't know if I ever had a fair shake in this so-called relationship now that I think about it. This nigga switched up and turned into this nurturing and loving man during my pregnancy, and that was enough to make me place all my trust back into him again. I'm talking he was doing it all, rubbing my feet and massaging my back. During one of his *I'm-all-in* days of course, I remember when we stayed in bed and loved on each other all damn day. I mean, I was really feeling his excitement about the whole new baby and family thing! On the other hand there were times I would call and get no answer or be waiting up until 2 a.m. on his ass!

*****

Thinking back on all this shit makes me realize just how much I took from him. I can remember this particular night I was reading *The Hottest Summer Ever Known,* because I loved to read while I was pregnant, and here comes this drunk ass nigga walking in late as fuck, loud and irritating as hell! A pregnant bitch is one of the worst bitches to piss off. We are very sensitive and almost anything can irritate us. A nigga can chew too loud and aggravate us, so one could only imagine how I was feeling as I was sitting there knocked the fuck up, but not really showing at this time. To add gas to the fire all that fun time was over for me because I was pregnant, which meant a bitch couldn't drink nor do some of the partying things I had grown accustomed to doing!

So here comes this nigga Will and his friend's loud and obnoxious asses into our castle with all that fuckin noise after leaving the strip club, and not answering my calls for *hours*. He had a bitch ready to commit a purge! But, I had to wooosah on this nigga right then. He walked his happy ass upstairs yelling out loud,

"HEY BABY, how are my two babies!!" His drunken sloppy ass fell down on the bed trying to lay his head against my stomach, making an attempt to kiss my belly button and I SNAPPED!

"Nigga! You would know how your two babies was doing if you would have answered your fucking phone!"

He goes on to tell some bullshit ass lie that I've heard many times before. It was at the point that I started to care less more and more. Though this night in particular my hormones were raging or something, because I could not turn my 'I DONT GIVE A FUCK' button on, I swear. The lies were written all over the wall, the embarrassment and disrespect was not enough to break the love I had for him. I was pissed the fuck off but not going anywhere. I wanted to dig a little to see what this nigga was hiding. On some real shit, I wasn't the type to check nigga's phones and shit, but, with the baby thing and all the extras a bitch had been through with him, I couldn't wait for his ass to go to sleep! I knew his drunk ass wouldn't hear a thing anyway!

All of his boys had bounced and Will had finally fell asleep, mouth wide open. As the sounds of his annoying snores roared though our bedroom, I knew it was time to play Inspector Gadget. I walked over to his pants to reach for his phone and what the fuck did I find? A 3-pack of condoms, with 2 left! Well, bitch where was the third one? It was obvious he had used one of them and it was at that point I was fuming! I politely left the 2 condoms on a pillow with a note that said: *"Gone to Miami looking for the third condom!!"* and I bounced.

The last thing a nigga wants is another nigga fuckin his bitch. Shit, I had to get my mind right so I called up my girls Robin & Tia.

"Bitches! Ain't Miami where the niggas throw the dick?" They laughed.

"What did he do bitch!" Robin asked giggling at my Uncle Luke comment.

"Irrelevant. I'm ready to roll the fuck out. Get ready!"

They were excited, of course. We hadn't hung out in a while since I had been under this nigga's surveillance. It was time for a change of environment and what better way to make some shit pop off right then, but to hang out in Miami! My ass was so anxious to leave I didn't waste no time getting the fuck on up out the D. I was fucking miserable and I needed to breathe some new air in a new environment.

Tia was the one who always kept a job out of all my friends so it wasn't as easy for her to get away. They wouldn't give her the days off, and I needed my girls right now! My mind was fucked up. I can't stand a cheating ass nigga. And I'm pregnant too DAMN!! I was barely showing so I did not give a damn. I was gonna make it happen baby bump and all. Tia said Sam had pulled some slick shit on her just like Will's punk ass did me. It was enough for her to say fuck that job, and that she'd apply for another one while we were on vacation. She was a nurse and knew she'd be back working by the next week.

"You know I love you F and ain't no way in the world I'm not going to be there for my bestie when she needs me!!" Tia said with excitement, I almost cried.

Real bitches cry real tears. These were my ride or die bitches!!

As I was preparing to make my move, I went down to the safe and grabbed $100,000 in all $100 bills. Me, Tia, Nicky and Robin hit Miami with stacks of $100 bills tucked tight between our legs and in between 2 pairs of panties and a pad to avoid it showing up through airline security. Nicky was my home girl. She was cool and funny as hell.

The crazy part was that $100,000 seemed like a lot right? WE SPENT THAT SHIT QUICK!! We were VIP everywhere we went! We hung out with people like Diddy, Busta Rhymes, Wu-Tang Clan, Nelly, Lil Wayne, Kelly Rowland - the list goes on and on! Bottles after bottles!! We were living the life of celebrities outside of the D, away from the drama and bullshit. After a great night we headed back to our room and Tia's phone was ringing off the hook! We were all cracking up at her ass knowing who was on the other end of her phone riding her coat tails - her dude Sam.

"Nigga DAYUM, can't a bitch have fun in Miami with my girls? I think you're stalking me!" She teased him, giggling.

"It ain't no fun when the rabbit got the gun," she said to piss him off.

That's when her smile turned into a frown after he told her that someone broke into their crib! They had just moved a few months ago and very few people had even been to their house because of the crazy robbery incident on Thanksgiving.

Honestly, they were both very blessed to have escaped that shit! I was a little confused Sam was not supposed to leave the house at night period. Someone was supposed to always be there! Shit, it was money and work there! They agreed to make sure someone would always be there with the heat to protect what's mine! Tia was with me in Miami which meant it was Sam's job to be there. I guess they said fuck the rules because they were mad that we jetted on their asses. As usual, they went to their favorite spot - the strip bar. They ended up staying only for an hour but still! Hell, in that hour they got 800 lbs and $300,000 in cash stolen, all because they didn't follow the MUTHAFUCKIN' PLAN!

Like they say, never send your child swimming with anyone because no one will watch them like you will. That's how I felt about my shit; no one is going to protect my shit like me bottom line. Another reason why I felt niggas wasn't bent out of shape like I was - the fact that it wasn't their loss, it was mine!! That's where this old saying comes to play – If you want something done right you have to do it yourself! I couldn't sleep all night! I didn't wanna be in Miami, I did not want to be in the "D" either. I wanted my shit back though, and that's all the fuck I wanted. All I could think about was what have I done so wrong for all of these fucked up things to keep happening to me like this. Shit, they say more money more problems, hell, I'm starting to believe that shit! The bad side to this beautiful hustle was paying me visits a little too frequent.

The sun was rising and Tia, Nicky and Robin woke up to find me still sitting in the same chair as the night before in my beautiful dress and makeup still flawless, but with this emptiest look. I was frozen.

"What's wrong F?" Tia asked concerned.

"Just in deep thought, that's all." I replied sounding real dry.

"Talk to me best friend. I hate seeing you like this," she asked

"I'll sum it up for you. There are two things you don't mess with when it comes to me. My family and my money. Period." I said slowly to make sure everyone understood the severity of what the fuck just happened.

They just kind of stared at me and each other like, *'Where did that shit come from?'* That's how I was. I would leave muthafuckas in suspense, which would eventually reveal the fucked up muthafuckas for who they really are. The fun was over, and we all made our way back home to our everyday problems. Back to reality! Shit hadn't really changed on my end, but life went on, and it wasn't long before my anticipated life changing moment presented itself. My first born was about to make her appearance very soon. It was time to focus on my new baby, a new attitude, and most importantly, making better decisions.

25

"The Ying To My Yang"

I tried to forget about the problems we were having, and focus more on my two girls. Fanesse made her debut to the world and her big sister was there to welcome her. They were like my rocks. I knew sooner or later I would have to pry Fanesse away from the nipple and take my ass back to the streets. There were absolutely no exceptions to the rule! Will left me no choice than to make room for our other companies that were making that legitimate paper. Hell, life had to go on, not to mention things started getting worse financially, but, if there was a 'will' (not the hubby, just to clarify) there was a way! I'm a bitch that can bounce back with the quickness! A new day and a new hour, and I had transformed like one of those super-hero bitches I used to watch when I was a kid! I was ready to hit the bricks and re-stack the chips!

I got Fanesse set up in a really good high profile daycare center over in Birmingham where everybody who is somebody took their child. Though I was in a different line of business, no one could tell. My money spent just like theirs, my new bundle of joy was just as precious as theirs and I participated just like they legally rich asses. I attended some of the social groups with the parents who happened to be judges, attorneys, doctors, Bentley dealers, executives and even presidents of the big 3! I always made sure the kids were well kept and secure. Both Fanesse and

Alexis never went without, even if I had to sacrifice my own personal shit to make sure private school and day care was paid in full every week! Fuck that! I wanted the best for mines and would walk to the end of the earth if it meant securing their future.

I had this burst of energy that came out of nowhere! I had my connects on speed-dial, and was all over them once the coast was clear! I never did business with my kids around. You got some bitches out here that lack parenting ethics. They smoke weed around their kids, fuck, curse and fight in front of them. These young-kids-having-kids-BettyBoo-JerrySpringer-Reality-TV-watching-with-their-kids-bitches that call themselves Mothers and will allow all kinds of crazy shit to transpire in front of their kids. Not ya girl tho'. My family is my family and my business is my business. Although they were both very important to me, I always kept that shit separate.

I flipped my phone open, hit up my connect and got some shit poppin' quick! Before I knew it I had things up and rolling again as I hung up the phone with a smile from ear to ear. The one thing I was hoping for was forgiveness from the connect. Could I be forgiven for all of Will's fuck ups? Hell, one thing they knew was this hoe was loyal; I can only vouch for me, but I'm talking 4 muthafuckn' years of gettin' money with these cats and never once did they have to go behind me on shit! They perfectly understood and were ready to get back to work. I was so ready to get back to AZ the following month! The adrenalin was crazy and the money to be made was only a few miles away! I had two mouths to feed.

My phone is like my lifeline. That muthafucka rings so much one would think I'm running a telemarketing service! Like now, Robin ass calling me probably because I didn't call her back! Hell, me and Will were into it because of me deciding to go out of town without him to AZ. One thing led to another and a bitch needed a break away from everyone.

"What's up Best friend!" I answered hoping that she didn't take me down that '*Bitch why the fuck you didn't call me back!*' road.

"You already know I'm about to curse yo' ass out right!" She said as she clearly displayed the fact that she was in her feelings.

"I'm sorry best friend. What's good?" I asked.

"Not a damn thing. I was calling to tell your ass about this dike that was trying to holler at me and I damn near back handed her ass on a reflex!"

"You know you wanted to show love." I teased her knowing how she felt about the whole gay thing.

"You know I am big on the to-each-his-own thing, but, when you step to me looking like a deformed nigga with a bandanna on, pants saggin and a fuckin tooth pick hanging from your mouth, I wanted to cringe! Why can't these women who want to live that lifestyle maintain their appearance? They ain't got to be doing all that extra shit for attention. I hate that shit!"

"You made your point." I said

"You not listening to me Fauna." She snapped

"I am. Some dude just pulled up on the side of me playing one of Blade's songs.... Dayum, I swear, hearing that shit brings back all kind of memories" I told her.

"Yeah, I miss his crazy ass too. I don't know if I'm more mad I didn't give him no pussy, or the fact that he didn't get a chance to make it. All that talent that nigga had and it was snatched away in the blink of an eye," she explained.

"Yea, that shit was too crazy…"

26

"Good People"

For those who haven't had the chance to experience Detroit, consider me the ambassador, taking you on a journey through my city. This is where I lay my head; this is where I call "home". My city represents a lot of things. For starters the D is complimented by many great and talented people who got their fair shot, but unfortunately lost their battle to the streets. For example, Blade Icewood, one of Detroit's most talented rappers who was also down with the group *Street Lords*. He was riding around here gettin' it. Fuck what you heard about all the killings, robberies, rapes and craziness that may happen on a day-to-day basis here in the D. You would honestly have to live here to know that we are so much more. For many years the media portrayed us as one of the worst cities, but no matter what you want to believe, we are far from it.

We're not the only city filled with drug dealers, killers, liars and cheaters! No matter where you go on this earth you will find one or two of those groups in any fuckin city. Watch enough of the ID Channel and you will learn that! Unfortunately, there will always be jealousy and rivalry here in the D. I know it's crazy. I can tell you about the people who are well mannered, speak and hold doors. I can tell you about the night life, the downtown city lights and them damn casinos. The city lights highlight the natural beauty. Then on the other hand I can tell you a million and one stories about all the good niggas gone, from a bullet to the dome, at the hands of a man or sometimes a woman filled with jealousy and hate. Every hood got a story, the makeshift memorials are scattered throughout the city. It's sad but it's so true which brings me to this profound story.

I often wondered if he woulda made it to perform at the BET Hip Hop Awards. Actually, I don't have to wonder, because I know he would of been on that stage reppin his city. His name is Darnell Lindsey, aka, Blade Icewood. We met back in the day at Maxis, the hottest nightclub during that time. Robin and I just so happen to bump into him as we made our way to the bar. This night I was hot and ready like Little Caesars pizza. Me and Robin grabbed two seats and sat our bags on the bar. I kept my eyes on everything. I looked to my left and slowly to my right as I bobbed my head to the beat. I glanced at this huge mirror behind the bar that ran into the ceiling. It was perfect, like eyes in the back of my head. The party was jumping. Our drinks came and we were having a good time when this young buck stepped to us saying,

"*DAAAMN!*" He took a step back and gave us a once over, licking his lips.

"Hey, what's up?" I responded kinda dry, taking a sip of my drink in between words, appearing uninterested at first. Robin gave him a head nod scanning the club to see if she saw anyone she knew. I knew from the expression on his face he felt played, he damn near went into shock. I guess he was thinking '*These stuck up hoes*', which we really weren't. It was his approach. Guys try to holla at us all the time. We were fine and always fresh as fuck. The girls that stood out in the club, yep that's us. So please don't come with some mediocre ass shit we heard about an hour ago from some other dude. I would sometimes come off as nonchalant to guys that stepped to me with all the extra dramatics. Regardless of how you judge me from the outside, I am honestly a down to earth chick that's cool as fuck. Unfortunately, not too many people get close enough to me to see that side. Sometimes they blow it at their first breath. I can't stand no funky breath, fucked up ass teeth nigga. I just can't and I don't think I'm asking for too much. Also, I prefer a nigga to be upfront and at least have good conversation. Niggas say all types of shit to me all the time and usually I just get over it and walk away. But us being unbothered by his comment seemed to make him very uneasy. This guy was a little different. He didn't just take the dis and leave, he continued to pursue us, but he was smooth about it. He posted up right behind us. The waitress came; he paid for our drinks and turned back around. Our backs were to his as we faced the bar. I glanced in the mirror and noticed how people started flocking around him, not to mention he cashed out countless drinks for us. Ok, now you got my attention just a lil bit. As the night went on we turned our seats to face the crowd that had formed near us. Soon after he stepped to my left and leaned down to whisper in my ear. He went from introducing himself as "Blade" to *'Oh damn you look good Ma'* to *"I'm out here trying to get it!"* Now that's what I was talking about! He was young and trying to get it. I mean this guy came equipped with drive and ambition. From that single conversation I knew he was someone that I would keep in touch with. But nobody could tell me that after sharing a few war stories and name-dropping at a club on a random night that he would turn into a lifelong friend.

That night was just the beginning. We would bump into each other off and on becoming closer as friends. As a matter of fact, I could remember several occasions we would hook up at his crib or ours and just blow. I mean bloooowww! He was one cool ass nigga. I remember Blade hit me up telling me to pull up on him because he had something on the floor. Me and my girls wasn't doing shit so we hopped in the car, rolled up and rolled out. I always pulled up on him ready to smoke first and foremost. He rolled down the window flashing that sexy ass smile.

"Yo, Fauna! Check this shit out baby!"

We all got out and walked over to his Rover. I could hear his voice bumping out the speakers. I could tell he was so into the idea of me and my girls being one of the first to hear his music. He excitedly flipped through the tracks going word for word, dancing and all. We had a private concert in his ride. That shit banged too, thank God because I would have hated to crush his spirit if the shit sounded wack. I was one of those kinda bitches that would say what was on my mind. I didn't sugar coat shit!

"Oh … My … Gawd! When you do that B?" I inquired rocking my hips from side to side. "That shit hot nigga." I graced my tongue across the outline of the cigar paper preparing to roll up, as my girls were holding up their red plastic cups filled with liquor!

"Please don't drop that alcohol!" Thinking about that new *Beyonce 7_11* at the thought of us holding up our red cups like lighters representing peace. *How ironic?* We had a buzz so strong! I swear it was a good day chilling with Blade flowing to his music.

"My shit is fire!" Blade threw his hands up waving them in the air, feeling his vibe.

That day we all smoked, choked, and joked around on how fake and jealous niggas were of him and his team's success out here in the streets of Detroit. We had a party in his Rover. The vibe is always right when you are in the company of good people.

"Bro, you know that if it ain't a nigga out here showing more hate than love you wouldn't be as successful as you are. You know that mean one fuck'n thing… keep doing what you doing!" I said passing him the blunt.

He stared off in to a deep thought still nodding his head back and forth to the music roaring from his truck. The music blasted as we bent a few corners throughout the neighborhood. That look in his eyes was a look of something dark, something deep. Something he probably wanted to tell us but probably couldn't. I could almost feel it. I didn't want to pry so I just leaned the passenger seat back in his truck giggling at my girls who had a buzz out of this world. They were in the back seat but was rocking like they were in VIP. The mood was so right. I fixed my hair in the mirror and rocked my head side to side to the music and fell carelessly into the zone with them.

It was time to get dressed and start my day. I popped in my Blade CD while I got myself together. *Damn it's hot today!* I thought to myself as I stepped out my front door hitting the pavement in my 5 inch heels. The sun was so hot I could feel it burning against my skin. It didn't matter because a bitch was looking good as usual. I felt like NuNu in the movie ATL in that scene when her and her girls went to the pool. Fine as hell. I mean, I was picture perfect this particular day with my big hoop gold diamond cut earrings dangling from my ears, gracing my tongue across my glossy red lipstick that matched my drop top apple-red Lexus on red spinners. The way the chrome on my rims sparkled along with the diamonds around my neck and wrist made me look like I was competing with the sun. I was shining so bright I could see my reflection clear as day on my beaming car. I swayed my hips as I checked myself out.   My tank top hugged my body and complimented my tightly fitted designer booty shorts. I threw on my shades, time to roll, I was ready for *whatever*.

It was the perfect summer day in the D, which was rare. The wind just right, the sun beaming and the breeze seemed to grace me at the perfect time. I can't stand Detroit weather, but no matter how crazy it can be, we always find ourselves back at this place we called home. The weather can take a turn for the worse at any given time. Just like a nigga. One day it could be up in the ninety's and the next it'll be freezing cold. I had just checked the weather the day before and it said it would be around 79ish, cloudy with a slight chance of rain. That bitch Mother Nature be on some bull. It was hot as hell! That's why this day was so peculiar. It was one of those days no one expected the weather to be as hot as it was. The sun was beaming against my bling and I was ready to hang with my girls. Jumping in my whip that was moaning out my name, I popped in Blades CD and raced off to meet my girls. We all hooked up at Robin's house, and then off to Red Lobster. I love seafood! It was one of my favorite spots and it was close, right there in Southfield before they closed it down because some fools got into it and shot up the place. The city of Detroit is rough but some niggas have no problem traveling to the suburbs either.

I pulled up to Robin's spot and they all jumped in with me and we headed down Telegraph looking good as hell! Them Charlie's Angels bitches ain't have shit on Detroit's Angel's! Niggas was riding up on us every other car and the hoes. The way they were staring at us burned holes in our shoulders. The only thing I could say to their hatin' ass was, "You mad or nah?!" I yelled out loud as we sat at the stop light for them to hear. They sped off damn near killing themselves not noticing the light was still red. Dumb asses! I guess they should have been mad driving up on us in their beat up cars, and it definitely was enough to make anyone lose sight of what was going on in front of them. Hell, I probably would have driven off too!

Turning off Telegraph heading up 7 mile, which was one of the city's hot spots during this time, everyone was out this day! It was bumper to bumper! Robin's phone kept going off and being that it was so many muthafuckas in our face, she kept ignoring the call until they became overwhelming. It was her baby Daddy calling. I saw this look on her face that forced me to pay so much more attention to her than the cars in front of me. I could tell whatever he was telling her was awful. So many things ran through my mind I almost ran into the back of a car multiple times from trying to get her attention. I needed her to tell me what was wrong. That's when she looked over at me, turned down my music and released this nervous sigh, something so painful I had to pull over.

It was my good friend - Darnell Lindsey aka Blade Icewood. He had been killed. He was gunned down on the same fucking street we were cruising on at one of the city's most popular car washes. Here I thought 7 mile was bumper to bumper because the weather was hot and niggas wanted to floss their new shit and pick up on some easy fuck shit. I would have never thought traffic was being held up because this niggas lifeless body was laid out for everybody to see. The muthafuckin D. It was a sad day for the city. Not only had we lost a good man, we lost one of the most promising possibilities for our city. He was a brother coming out of Detroit on his way to the top in the music industry. Many of us also lost a real friend.

When we rode past and saw all the yellow tape roping off the scene where he was, that was confirmation for us. His silver Range Rover with multiple bullet holes in it sat there on the side street with him still inside. It was like a horror film. We were just with him. We were just cruising that same street, hell we were just sitting in his truck. My heart dropped as I was thinking *damn*, just to think all of this shit was over some fucking lyrics to some song. At least that's what the word in the streets was. I couldn't believe some words was the reason why he was killed. I was sure there was more to that story but no one could ever explain why one would have to die over shit like this. There have always been rules and levels to this street shit. Now if a nigga set you up, harmed your family, threatened the lives of your loved ones or those close to you that may warrant this kind of action but, something like this really didn't make any sense. His untimely death was unnecessary and reminded me of the Tupac and Biggie West Coast and East Coast rivalry. Just like Pac, this was not the first time they tried to kill Blade.

I can remember like it was yesterday talking to Blade after the first attempt on his life about a year earlier over at his home in the middle of the night. Not only did he almost lose his wife in the midst of that crazy shit, he ended up paralyzed behind it. In an attempt to save her, the bullets hit his spine and from that point he was never able to walk again. These niggas was so bold they ran up in his shit in Oak Park where the police out there ain't got shit else to do *but* to respond within seconds! I told you them niggas have no issue with bringing their problems to the suburbs. Yet I was still shocked that someone had been so bold to go out there to attempt to kill him! How the fuck were they able to escape that fast! That was a mystery to everyone who had heard about it.

But, that nigga survived that shit, bullet wounds and all. He underwent the best care, being flown out of the country to see some of the top specialists to help him walk again, thanks to his Dad who was a strong support system in his life. He loved his son and wanted him to regain everything he had lost after that shit. I honestly saw Blade improving physically and on a serious come back which placed the idea of someone making another attempt on his life a possibility, in the back of my mind. I am from here, I know how they think. I have been through so much and seen even more that I have somewhat become desensitized to the horrible stories. Trust me, I have a heart but when that shit come back to back and get closer and closer, it turns you into a more guarded person. Watching every move and trusting nobody. Blade was on his way to a full recovery when he put out a new record. Everybody and they Momma was talking about that shit! That's all you would hear when you rode past someone in the streets was them bumping that shit! I wonder if he knew it would cause all hell to break loose! It was one of the hottest songs out then, and that had really pissed some nigga off. Those lyrics were obviously enough to make a muthafucka mad enough to want to see him dead.

Was it really worth it?

What I couldn't understand was why the fuck couldn't a muthafucka just write a comeback song, and kiss and make up while counting their chips. It was just music. That's how *real* muthafuckas about their paper would do! That's how you knew this was some bitch shit! All I could do was wonder,

"WTF was the world coming too!"

That nigga will always be one of the realist rappers that ever came out of the D to me.

Love you Darnell "Blade Icewood' Lindsey and may you rest in peace Bro.

27

"The Ninth Hour"

After having Fanesse, I was surprised how fast I bounced back. I was blessed with not losing my ass and tits, but my stomach seemed even tighter than it was before I got pregnant! No working out, no trainers after all that pregnancy shit, and I can honestly say that I was ready to take back what I had already started in the streets.

Being in the kind of game I was in had its ups and down and ins and outs. I guess I had been out of the loop for so long I got a little rusty under the nails. Not that I don't know how to get that bread; it was the drive I had that I felt myself becoming a little bored with. I had to find other shit to do in order to make up for some of the things I lacked. I was at my best when working in entertainment. Outside of the dope game being my number one stunner, throwing parties was what really had my name popping off! Before I knew it, I was being hired to show up and blow up at all kinds of events. Say my name, and that would bring the whole city out. It wasn't long before I was raking in major chips each time I threw a gig! I had sell out events at strip bars, clubs, and private parties. This was definitely one of my callings that I enjoyed a lot. I hung out with all the entertainers when they came to town, making a killing at the door and a percentage at the bar, life was good! Any kind of hustle is good.

I remember back when I was still in high school when I first jumped into this kind of shit. Though my hustle selling dope was in effect as early as my teenage years, I was raking in major chips for a young pretty bitch from the D, just by doing a few gigs around the city. This one particular event was one I would never forget. It changed the way I saw the stripper game, real talk. I had a cousin named Freddy that was always good with the ladies as much as I was good with the fellas. Like him, I always had a bunch of guys flocking around me hoping that one day they may have their opportunity with me. Of course I took full advantage of that by allowing them to have their fantasy, but never giving into them. That gave me complete control over them muthafuckas, allowing me to get whatever I wanted. I loved the attention, believe that. I just never let it go to my head.

This one time we were all hanging out in my Nana's basement pondering on this idea that ultimately paid off in the end. The plan was set in motion that Freddy would bring some strippers, and I would bring the niggas to spend the money! Nana had a nice layout that fit our plan with the full bar and a BOOM BOOM ROOM! The way we had it set up was the girls would pay $40 to dance, while the guys were given a cover charge of $20 to get in. Money rolled in easy especially with the grand idea of selling some fried chicken and spaghetti for a bunch of hungry/horny/high and fat muthafuckas with nothing to do but to outshine one another. We had blunts and condoms on deck! Shit, we had all kind of shit for sale and that shit slammed! At the end of the night we made good money and had a good time.

A few months went by of throwing our Friday night gigs and we noticed it started dying down! We couldn't

179

have that. We had to put our heads together and figure out how we could improve our numbers ASAP! I sat back, blazed a blunt and went into a deep thought on ways to keep this shit going. Then something clicked! We needed a highlight every week so we did things such as put plastic down and covered it with oil and let them hoes fight! Naw, fa'real tho'! It was like wrestling naked and that shit was so fun and entertaining, the numbers increased overnight! Before I knew it, we had a giant pool set up in the center of the floor for the strippers to bathe each other. These niggaz was so loving the new ideas, and before we knew it we were back on and poppin! It was my goal to have something popping off every week to entertain our guests. I was creative when it came to this kind of shit so stumbling up on something hot and new was what I set out to do. That's when I was introduced to this one woman named Reign that was the HEADLINER SHOW!!

The bitch Reign had a defect or something because I could never understand how she did some of the shit she was able to do! This bitch must be on layoff from the circus or something. I mean it was some real Shrine circus shit mixed with some Universoul shit! This one particular night the chick that introduced us brought her by. Me and my girls were getting set up for our night and were already buzz'n and anxious to see what the girl was bragging about so when they came through the timing was perfect.

"Hey Casey!" I greeted them at the side door escorting them down to the basement area at my Nana's where we held the jump-off parties.

"Hey Fauna. This my girl Reign!"

"Hey Sweetie!" Reign spoke with this overly high-pitched tone that pierced my damn ears.

"Okay okay... I'm good." I spoke looking her over.
She was very weird looking but interesting enough
to see what she was working with.

"Alright y'all let's get it crackin'!" I smacked my
hands together taking a seat folding my arms positioning
myself to watch the performance.

What I was expecting wasn't at all what happened
before my eyes. I had already been told the chick was
amazing. My errand boy Andre dimmed the lights. That
really made it easier on the eyes as this not-so-cute chick
did her thang. I was really being nice. We all stared in awe
at Reign as she started to prepare us for this killa
performance I kept hearing about that is supposed to be so
mind blowing! I stared at her intensely as she approached
the center of the floor and my mind went to wondering,

*I know this can't be the bitch everybody wanted me
to bring in!*

I fought to muffle my giggles as she started swaying
her hips bending it over, poppin and droppn' it. But wait,
then, I had only turned my head for a half of a second when
my eyes met a naked ass Reign who had stripped down to
nothing. I'm talking BUTT ASS NAKED! I guess she
noticed how intrigued I was at what she had done so far
that she became even more comfortable with her body.

She laid back on a table, put both her legs all the
way back behind her ears and started pushing in and out!
Now at this point I'm looking around the room to see if
everyone was thinking what I was – '*What... the
FUUUCK?!*'

Everyone had their mouths open and their eyes
pinned to the pussy! The way she was applying pressure to
the entire lower area made me wonder was the bitch

preparing for delivery! Before I could give myself time to figure out what her next move was, out came what appeared to be this small candy cane fighting its way through the deep dark hole of her pussy! I fell back in my chair yelling,

"HELL NAW!"

The room was in uproar! The look on Freddy's face was unexplainable. I nudged my partner as we both fell out laughing.

"FAUNA! FAUNA!" He screamed like a bitch!

It kind of startled me at first till I saw why. This bitch pussy was *Reigning* fucking candy canes like a gawd damn Christmas tree! She went from one to a dozen of them muthafuckas! I'm not done by far.

'Did this bitch just push out a toy bunny?'

After that came an Easter egg and then a few bullets that came out vibrating. Then a peppermint, wait...a peppermint? I noticed it was attached to a string. She was very creative. Like I said, she wasn't the prettiest bitch I've seen naked, but she was one of the most talented by far. I loved the way she interacted with her audience. Though it was just us, she made me feel like it was a room filled with people having a fucking ball. I knew by the reaction she was getting from my own circle, a room filled with strangers would pull in a lot of dough. BITCH! YA HIRED!

"Fauna...what the fuck was that I just saw?" My home girl was still fucked up over Reign's performance.

"No bitch! Did you see how much shit she had stored up in her pussy? Where they do that at?"

We were talking about that shit for hours later like a hot ass movie. At that point I was so outdone I wanted to

show and fucking tell what I had just seen! Then she asked
Freddy to turn the lights off and within a few seconds a
flashlight started shining, not just shining but she was
turning it off and on!!!... now ask me where did that come
from?... you guessed it... her pussy!!

She had to have some kind of compartment set up in
her uterus or something!! Possibly a lil midget in there
tossing the shit out. I couldn't even tell you which was the
craziest thing coming out of her pussy, because they all
were crazy!! I had to ask myself over and over again.

'*Was it the flashlight she pushed out and was able
to turn off and on?*

I could have thought of a number of ways she made
all that shit possible, but was I capable of doing it? Hell no!
The only thing besides blood and babies that is pushed out
of my pussy was on the sleazy, sexy horny side and that
was my nigga's nut when he would leave me filled with his
cum.

So, I wasn't a stranger to the kinky side of this
game. Her pulling out a big ass glass dildo telling me to
come look inside the glass dildo while it was in her was
some deep shit. It may have freaked the average bitch out.
Me? Ah no. This was what I do! I made all kind of shit
happen for all kind of muthafuckas. Now at first I was a
little apprehensive not really wanting to participate. But,
what I had to realize was my participation would attract
everyone else's attention and was one fa'sho way to make
my bread by that ninth hour.

28

"Pause"

Growing up, I really had no complaints as far as me doing what I wanted to do. Like I mentioned before, I had a great loving Mom and Dad and no matter what my Nana always held me down without judgment. I could go to her whenever I wanted to talk about things. I felt more comfortable opening up to her, when I couldn't bring myself to discuss certain things with my Mom. They were two entirely different animals when it came to advice. I strived for that same relationship with my girls. I would do whatever it took to protect them. I wanted it even more after what happened to the daughter of one of the dancers who worked at one of my Promoter's gigs!

Marini was the dancer's name. She was very quiet and reserved. A young chick that made her money, and got the fuck on after every performance. I just thought maybe she was about her bread, and possibly had a man at home she had to get to. I was dead wrong. I am very observant and noticed her sitting off to herself. It was one of my slappin' nights but she appeared a little depressed. I pulled her to the side.

"Hey girl are you alright?" I asked her with deep concern.

I could see in her face something was bothering her that was serious, not to mention she wasn't poppin her ass on a night that was packed with paid niggaz everywhere! Something had to be wrong. She told me her male cousin who was 19 years old had been molesting both her kids while she was at work! She was very distraught and afraid, not only for what happened to her babies, but what might happen to her kids if her baby daddy found out. There was no doubt she would lose custody of them. I wanted to kill that nigga for her, and I didn't really know her at all! I just felt so bad for her. She was different from the regular hoes that worked after work (turned tricks). She did her job, always talked about her kids and hurried home to them every damn night. It's always the bitches that try to do right who always seem to catch the bad deals. I did what I could to help her out and she was able to put herself in a better environment to raise her kids in.

The whole situation forced me to reflect. I lit my blunt hoping the blunt would cloud the bad images in my mind. As bad as I wanted to ignore what happened to me when I was young, that situation forced me to relive it. It started one day when I was hanging out with my Mom and my sister at one of their cleaning jobs. My Mom worked for this very handsome man who I looked up to. I thought the world of him. He was something like my idol and for him to strip me of my dignity and steal my self-worth was immoral. I held him solely responsible for some of the insecurities that I endured with men in my life!

I would always ask myself, *'Have I forgiven him, grown past the things he had done to me?'* I tapped into my inner child to branch out and face this nightmare from my past with the hopes that it wouldn't haunt me for life. I remember looking at this slick nickel-dime nigga in a well-creased suit, saying how much I wanted my husband to be just like him - a CEO of his own company and well mannered. He was a very close friend of the family. My Mom only worked for him because he was a close friend of the family and needed her assistance on a temporary basis until he found someone more permanent. So she decided to help out and make a few dollars in the process. He was well dressed and a very successful man that was driven by this deep-rooted talent he was blessed with. Oh, and did I say he was a *very* nice looking brotha too, could of made the cover of GQ magazine. My young mind adored his every footstep which made the situation even worse.

My Mom worked for him and my sister ended up working for him also. So, when he would hug me and give me this pat on my ass as to say 'great job' on whatever task I was working on at the time, I really didn't think much of it. I liked the smell of his cologne. I was only a kid so my thoughts on shit like that didn't process very quickly until that very day. It was what he had done and how I was feeling that got me thinking this wasn't right. I was only 12 when it first happened; even though I was fully developed physically I was still just a kid. I remember this so well it was like it just happened yesterday. Here is how it went down.

My Mom was downstairs cleaning and I was upstairs watching TV. I was one of those intense TV watching young teens that could recite damn near any show I liked at that time, verbatim. So there I was chillin' with my eyes glued to the screen when I heard the door creep open. I damn near broke my neck from turning it so fast in the direction of the noise that screeched from the door frame! I turn quickly to see who it was and thought, '*oh shit!*'! I looked around to see if I had dropped any crumbs on the floor from the sandwich and chips I just ate. Mom said not to make a mess. I wasn't clumsy, it was just one of those things I would unconsciously do when caught off guard. As my thoughts continued to roam I thought, *'It's my Mom's boss'.* I felt a little uneasy wondering why he would be coming into this room if my Mom was downstairs! *'Was he coming to watch some TV with me or...'*

Oh well, I brushed it off and continued to watch my program. Now you know how you could feel someone's eyes burning a hole in the back of your head? That's how it felt at that time. I felt his presence was there but the fact that he hadn't acknowledged himself was what had me wondering WTF he was up to. What was next? Him sitting there staring at me for what seemed like forever, had me a little nervous at that point so I got up and went to the bathroom. Moments later, BOOM! The door slung open! *'Damn!'* I thought as I stood at the sink looking at him with my face tensed up wanting to ask myself, *'Mom always said lock the door when I go to the bathroom, why didn't I lock the damn door!'* Then again, why would I? He didn't appear to be any threat to me at the time so the idea of locking my bathroom door didn't seem necessary. That was until his ass came barging in and pinned me against the sink! Before I could utter a word he had his tongue down my throat. I don't know what was worse, him kissing me like he was trying to surgically remove my tongue or him feeling on my barely developed breast! It was gross. The slob was the worst. I was so scared at the moment the only thing came to mind was getting his ass off of me! I didn't know what to do! I hated it. This had never happened to me before. What was crazy about what happened is when he continued I started having the feeling of wanting more! Shit, it felt kinda' good! I was experiencing this tingling feeling I had never felt before, but in the back of my mind I knew it wasn't right for this old ass man to be doing what he was doing to me. The only thing I could remember at that moment was me crying and he stopped instantly.

He had this look of regret in his eyes that read '*What the fuck did I just do?*' He made an attempt to wipe my tears while brushing his hand across my hair and caressing my shoulder with hopes of shushing me. "Hey, I'm so sorry." He pleaded lifting my chin up to meet him eye to eye. I just stared at him and remained silent. It was one of those "oops I fucked up'" moments he couldn't take back. "I promise if you accept my apology and keep this between us it will *never* happen again. *"Did I believe him?* I think right at that moment I may have wanted to, but it wasn't long after that first incident every time he found the right opportunity to target me again he was all over me. It was becoming so crazy he would go one step further each time. He even had the balls to feel on my bare private part areas! The parts Mom told me nobody should ever touch. The crying didn't matter anymore. Honestly, I felt like he had this sick idea that my cries may have been tears of passion. In the end, his ass didn't care. He began to bribe my young mind and he caressed my mature body. He would add extra pressure by saying each time, "If you want your Mom and sister to keep their jobs you better keep our secret."

He threatened me looking me in the eyes with my back against the wall in between his arms planted to hold his body weight. I felt trapped and his words were like a gun being pointed at my head. The fact of the matter was I knew how bad we needed the money and most importantly I didn't want my Mom or my sister to lose their job. Now part of me wonders if he called them to work or did he know them coming to work for him would bring an extra bonus, me. We needed the extra money so I felt obligated. I committed to him and his bullshit by allowing the shit to continue and not say anything. All kind of things went through my mind especially when he mentioned my sister. It made me wonder if he may have touched her too! Was she the initial target and I just happened to come along for the ride? Though she was much older than me, and prettier with a bombshell body that was fully developed, I couldn't see how he targeted me instead of her! I guess Chester the child molester would rather play with a child than a grown ass woman.

As months went by and he continued to fondle me I guess he was finally ready to walk me across his stage and give me his dick diploma. I don't know what made him think sticking his big ass anaconda dick in my mouth would be a good move on his part. I was a child. I was familiar with the kissing and touching, I use to sneak and watch it on TV. However, this move he just pulled was foreign and I knew for sure it was not right. Let me just say this! BLOOD WAS FUCKIN EVERYWHERE!!! As soon as his dumb ass inserted his flesh in my mouth I tried to rip it from his body with my teeth! I had never had a penis in my mouth and I didn't want it there, neither!

If I had known the only thing I had to do to put a stop to this was to break some skin, it would have happened way before then! He hated my guts after that. It was like a bad break up for him that left him like a sour ass apple. I went crazy on his ass to a point where he couldn't even look at me! Hell, I was happy and back to my usual shit, being a 12 year old child.

Unfortunately, he was the first but definitely not the last adult male figure to cross my line. Because of the experience I had with these male predators I knew how to handle them after that. I never told anyone, until now. It forced me to handle things in my own way, which could have been good or bad. To be clear and well understood, it was now my way or no way, period. Going through this made me wiser and very overprotective of my girls. I realize like any Mother, these kinds of boys and men can slide through the cracks like sheep in wolves clothing. I have seen many people catch hell behind shit like this! They blame their Mom for not protecting them, and even worse, it affects their future relationships.

I'm different. I'm one of those unique bitches that accept the bad for the bad and the good for the good. I carry no baggage into my relationships, and I don't take in any additional stress to avoid premature wrinkles. I have to be everything my Mom and Dad were to me for my kids, and that's being their strength by any means necessary. My Dad's love and devotion was one of the many reasons why I was able to get past what had happened to me. He showed me that there are good men in this world, with promise and loyalty. I know if I had not had that guidance and discipline growing up under his roof with his repeated "*I told you so*" and "*I ain't gon' tell you no wrong Fauna*", I wouldn't be half the woman I am today, flaws and all.

29

"Blink"

After flying in from AZ, I had to organize my bundles and get my schedule back on track. I hadn't called Mama Fran, who was watching the girls while I was out of town, to let her know I was back. Hell, I had been up for the last few days and was damn near in a zombie state when I touched down. I missed my girls and all, but I needed what energy I had left to get out in the streets before I punched back into Mommy mode that meant going back to my 24/7 home life. Back to business then off to get my babies.

After packaging up everything and making a few calls to set things in motion and while I was waiting on a few business calls, I hit up my BFF Tia for a brunch at the tittie bar. Just on some lunch date shit and play catch up on everything that had been going on in the D while I was away. Being that Will was in the streets like always, and who also didn't know I was home. I just wanted to know what muthafuckas was doing when they think Fauna's not in town. I knew she was the person to hit up for all the info.

Before I could get out my front door, this hoe was racing up in my circular driveway like a bat out of hell, music blasting and her annoying ass voice sounding like the cry of death from her fucking up the lyrics to one of Mary J. Blige's songs she was playing. She must have forgotten my bougie ass neighbors don't play that shit. She obviously had something planned because when she got to me the blunt was already rolled and her ass was on ten!

"Hey Bitch!" Tia yelled over the music.

"You know that's my shit!" I hollered, humming the notes to the song as I rocked my hips making my way to the car.

"You need to get yo' ass in this car right now'!" She gave me this *'got something to tell you'* look.

I didn't hesitate jumping in and turning down the music, she lit the blunt as we pulled off.

"Where we going?"

"You'll see!" Tia said passing me the blunt.

"That's what I'm talking about!" I took hold and pulled smoke into my fragile lungs releasing a deep yet sensational cough.

"I thought you had something juicy, the way you were talking over the phone." I stared at her, waiting anxiously on a response.

She had this look on her face that she knew something, but was hesitant.

"Fauna, when I tell you I hate bringing shit to you about your dude, I swear."

I tried to talk but the bitch cut me off. I hate when she does that shit!

"Wait wait! Let me finish!" Tia put her hand up.

"You and I both know how you are when it comes to Will. I have brought shit to you that only he knew I knew because I was the one who caught his ass in the act, and tell you, and what do you do? You confront him, go HAM and within a few days y'all back boo'd up and he be walking around mean muggin my ass!"

"Okay, you got a point. I don't know what kind of hold this nigga got on me fa'real." I said

"A dick hold bitch!" She yelled.

We laughed but that was cut short. I wanted to know what the fuck she knew so I continued to push her. We pulled up to an unfamiliar restaurant, not one I would have chosen that sat on the other side of Woodward off 7 mile.

"What the fuck is this? I don't eat Middle Eastern food! Shit nasty as hell, too much garlic," I said irritated as fuck because we still haven't got to the bottom of her story.

"It's not the food or the place I brought you here for. It's who's inside." She looked at me with a totally blank expression on her face that started to make me nervous. My buzz was fading away and it was hard for me to face unexpected shit if I'm not high.

Tia parked at the grocery store which was on the other side of the building. Giving us a little distance from the front of the building. "You ready?" she asked with the craziest look on her face.

"Bitch, I'm not about to go in there unless you tell me what the fuck is going on! You know how much I hate surprises!" I said folding my arms

"Oh, you're going to want to know what's behind door number 7 bitch, believe that! Come on!" Tia grabbed her Gucci bag and hopped out slamming the door. What the fuck, I thought to myself as I put the blunt out, grabbed my Chanel bag and hurried across the parking lot to catch up to Tia. Walking toward the half empty restaurant, the other businesses were overcrowded with Middle Eastern muthafuckas. I thought I was in Dearborn. It was so saturated that you could smell them musty muthafuckas before you crossed Woodward.

The sidewalk was full of litter, just nasty - the storefronts weren't maintained either. Please don't let me start on how the upkeep of their grocery store was. You can see how fucked up it is from outside the window. Imagine what it smelled like. Yuck! Every time I pictured one of these stanky ass rude muthafuckas, I imagined them digging in their noses or asses and handling my food without washing their hands! Them rude muthafuckas will do that to you. Don't get me wrong I got respect for the people of the Chaldean, Arabic and Lebanese community. Come to Detroit, you will be surprised. A lot of them get it like we get it but way better because they stick together. Some of the chicks got style too, they be in the latest shit, fly as fuck, looking like me. You know the niggas that got hustle in they blood like me and the chicks that's super cool and know about fashion and always on point. Hell they work like I worked, love the same shit I loved. After 9-11 America made them the new nigga, hated and harassed. In society's eyes, they were worse than niggas, so we got a lot in common, they cool with me. It's those funky smelling, rude ass muthafuckas I can't stand. It ain't about their heritage; I dislike any funky smelling rude muthafucka. It's most definitely NOT personal. It seemed like it took me an hour to take 15 steps. Yep, I counted them muthafuckas because I was not sure what the fuck I was about to walk into. It was like in the movie when the character is walking to meet their fate and the picture is slow and music damn near depressing. I just wasn't feeling my surroundings, but because it was my one and only friend I would ever trust to follow her into some shit like this, I was game.

"Wait Tia!" I said before she grabbed the door handle. "Come over here!" I said as I grabbed her pulling her away from the entrance. She walked around on my side insisting that I just follow her into this unknown territory.

"Okay look…" She exhaled out of breath from walking so fast. "Will and a very well known bitch we both know is in there eating. Now ask me how I know this?" She folded her arms tilting her hips to one side waiting on my response.

"Where is his truck?" I scanned the area that was absent of his vehicle. There was only what appeared to be a 1998 or 99' black Suburban and a couple older model cars I could count on my fingers in the broken concrete parking lot that sat beside several abandoned houses.

The feeling I was getting wasn't one I could really put into words. But whoever the bitch was he was caking with up in this rundown spot, couldn't have possibly been anyone I would call a friend or even an associate for that matter!

"Just tell me who she is and she will get dealt with'! I just hate not knowing what I am walking into Tia, you know how I am. I fucking hate surprises and you of all people should know this!"

"First let me tell you how I spotted dey' ass."

"Can they see us while we are clearly standing out in the open?" We outside plotting in front a glass front building. The windows were dirty as hell but shit we ain't actually invisible either. The whole scene just didn't feel right. Here we are standing in the heart of somewhere horrible. Obviously standing out in broad day light in $3,000 shoes, over $18,000 worth of what I called junk jewelry and my $9,000 Chanel bag I had just bought in AZ.

I don't even want to say how much the gear I was rockin cost. It was just not the place for a pretty bitch like me. Not to mention I may have to whoop a bitch ass! "All jokes aside." I snapped in this serious tone resting my hands on my hips. This shit was fucked up and for Tia to not have given me a heads up got me feeling some kind of way!

"You could have at least let me know what was up woman! Look at me! Do I look like I'm ready for some gangsta shit? I am too fly for this shit today. You could have told me and I would have put my Nikes on." Then I asked, "So are we going to just stand here and wait on these muthafuckas to walk out and see our dumb asses standing here, or are we going to walk in and confront them?" She shrugged her shoulders staring at me.

"Hold up..." I walked back to the car.

"What now damn?" she said annoyingly.

"Bitch just unlock this damn door so I can put my purse in here! I'm not about to knock a bitch out and have my purse in my hand! You know how much I paid for this bag? Look at you! You look like you ready to go upside someone's head with that jogging suit and gym shoes you got on." I stared her up and down as I sat my purse on the passenger seat opening it putting my jewelry inside.

"OOOMGEEEE! Can you come on already!" She said impatiently.

"Can you back off already? I'm not stepping in that hole-in-the-wall with all this shit on!" I rolled my eyes taking my bag and placing it behind my seat on the floor.

"Because the only thing this dick-sucking-gold-dign'-chicken-head bitch could possibly be doing with your husband is fucking him. You already know how she cut." Tia struggled with her words from being out of breath after sprinting across the parking lot to avoid some dumb ass nigga going 35mph in a parking lot, told you some of them muthafuckas be rude as fuck! If guns were legal, I swear I would have shot his ass, he almost hit us!

I was only a few feet away from finding out what was behind door 7. I had to know who this bitch was before I walked in.

I said, "wait now, either tell me who the bitch is NOW or I'm gon' whoop yo ass!"She took a deep sigh and said the name of someone that yanked my heart straight out of my chest!

"It's Robin." I politely slid Tia out the way and proceeded towards the door, damn near spraining my ankle from the shoes I was wearing! Before I could grab the handle Tia snatched my ass! We both looking like some damn fools playing outside of what was supposed to be a damn restaurant. Fuck that! I just learned my best friend is in there with my husband! All type of shit was going through my head. My purse and jewelry is in the car so Tia can take that to my Mom if I go to jail I was out for blood.

"WAIT FAUNA WAIT!" Tia said as she grabbed both my arms.

"OH! SO NOW YOU WANT ME TO WAIT!" I was breathing so hard trying to pry her fingers away from my arms.

"Listen for one minute! Just hear me out!" she pleaded.

I jerked away from her trying to catch my breath! "What?! HURRY THE FUCK UP WITH IT!" I kneeled over resting my hands on my knees looking up at her, out of breath, anxious and just all over the place. This bitch was taking too long to talk.

"Let's not just run up in the bitch like some ruthless ass niggas trying to get shot up before we step foot through that door fool! You got to think boo! This ain't Red Lobster muthafucka!"

She had a point there. This pissy ass smelling spot definitely wasn't no place of elegance, and now that I had time to process my reaction, I *was* on some double murder shit. I seen all the episodes of Snapped, I had that shit all planned out. "Okay whatever. So now what bitch! You talking about one of my best friends in their having a chit-chat with my muthafuckin husband, and we still sitting out here debating. What kind of shit you on Tia? Fa'real."

I was becoming extremely irritable by the second, being that she at one point was so turned up on the idea of kicking in the damn door, and now the bitch wanted to ditch the project mentality to practice proper etiquette. I was so damn confused. Tia wanted to assure me she was down but wanted to make sure we were safe. She explained, "I just want you to confront the situation, not get us sprayed up, that's all. These muthafuckas in here don't recognize our kind of drama. They women don't act like we do. They scared of their men. We come in that bitch like some angry black women we gone be on a t-shirt. I know you mad bitch, but let's be smart about this shit". Understanding her point I took a deep breath, fixed my clothes and said "Okay! You made your point. Now let's go!"

I made my way in first and she followed close behind me. What happened next only happens in gangsta movies. Two hood looking ass niggas came out from behind the wall that appeared to lead to some other area inside the empty shell of a restaurant.

At first I didn't know what was happening. It took me only a matter of seconds to put what was happening together. I turned to look at Tia, who was now standing on the side of me and I thought, *'Oh my God...this is not happening to me again...'*

"Okay! I got her here so now what!" Said Tia...my so-called best friend to some low-life niggas who obviously were plotting some bullshit! I felt so betrayed; this shit can't be going down. Not again, not my best friend. I was so furious that I couldn't hold back!

"YOU BIT....!" I started to yell.

That's when she slapped me across the face so hard I lost it! I blacked out! By the time I came back to reality, they had me duct taped and tied to a chair. I was in so much pain not only from the blows that were inflicted by both Tia and her busta-ass niggas that called themselves Big Po and Byrd, but the tape and rope was so tight I felt suffocated. I just wanted to wake up from this nightmare. How did I not see this coming? Is Sam in on this shit? Really Tia, I thought to myself? She just leaned against the wall that appeared to be under some kind of construction and stared at me with this envious smirk on her face. The whole time tears welled up in my eyes, because I wanted to understand how she could have done something so fucked up to me!

We did damn near everything together! Anything I had she had! Jewelry, expensive clothes, fancy trips you name it and POOF, she had it! I was good to that bitch, and that was one of the only reasons why I would have mustered up a tear over her sorry ass!

"WHAT THE FUCK ARE Y'ALL WAITING FOR?! CALL HIM!" yelled Tia.

"YOU NEED TO CALM DOWN A NOTCH BABY GIRL! All that yelling ain't gonna get the nigga on the phone any faster!" The guy Byrd snapped on her ass! My eyes were filled with tears, I couldn't see at all from my right eye. It was swollen and I could tell from the blood and pain, it was all fucked up. I couldn't say shit because of the duct tape around my mouth. All and all, I was fucked, by someone I grew to love and trust.

Once I calmed down, I started to think why am I still alive. What do they want? It didn't take long for me to figure out what their intentions were. I was being held for a million dollar ransom and Will was the bank they were attempting to pull from. I felt like I had been tucked away in a box for days as I could hear them arguing in another room about this money tip! I had never in my life been so afraid of what would happen when and if they did get their hands on that money! There was no doubt in my mind Will was going to pay it but the fact that I saw faces, and one of them was a very familiar one who just happened to be a once close acquaintance was just all bad at this point! That alone was enough to draw one conclusion; I wasn't getting out of this alive. The same feelings, thoughts, emotions and tears from the Cash Money Jay situation came back to pay me a visit.

As I sat in the dark closed in area I could hear Tia yelling and screaming! Those intense sounds forced me out of my death trance! I was constantly trying to break loose of the ropes around my wrist and ankles every chance I thought they weren't paying attention. Before I could make another attempt to get untangled I heard a gunshot followed by what sounded like someone falling to the floor! This shit was getting too familiar.

I noticed I never heard Tia's voice again after that neither. I was trying to force a scream that was muffled intensely by the tape around my mouth and the mucus that had formed in my nose. Here I sat hopeless. "I CAN'T BREATHE DAMMIT!" I yelled like my life depended on it, hoping and praying someone behind those gunshots would hear me because I was just only a few feet away! As the footsteps grew closer, my body muscles began to lock up! Then appearing out of the darkness was the guy Byrd.

He walked a little closer and said, "Just wanted to let you know we had to cancel your husband's contract along with ya girl in there. No need to break bread with the dead wouldn't you agree?" This sarcastic muthafucka was most definitely not gonna let me out of here alive. It was right at that very moment I saw my life flash before me as he raised his gun aiming it toward my head!

POW!! The bullet hit me in my head! It was like a hard piece of metal penetrating my brain and forcing its way through like a train traveling at full speed through a tight tunnel! I was dying in the middle of a vacant building floor, where no one would find my body for weeks, or possibly months! As my heartbeat began to slow up I could feel myself choking. That's when I went into this coughing frenzy in what felt like a strong stench of smoke smothering me. My mind started wondering as I could feel myself slowly drifting away. *'Had they set the place on fire?'* My babies were waiting on me. I hope someone finds out the truth. My parents will not understand, my babies will hurt forever, especially Lex. Then suddenly this familiar voice called out to me. "Fauna!" It was Will's voice. I must be in the final stages of death because it sounded like he was right next to me.

It was like I wanted to respond, but I felt paralyzed until he nudged me, waking my ass up out of my sleep and blowing weed smoke in my face. I jumped up in a cold sweat, looking around this familiar room that just so happened to be mine! In my own bed coming up out of some deep ass sleep, OH MY GOD!

The shit was only a fucking nightmare! Thank God! After packing everything up and making a few calls I must have passed out on the couch. My phone died so Will picked up the girls from Momma Fran, I forgot I told her I was back and would be there shortly. I was alive my babies were safe and I wake up to a kiss from my husband and a breakfast blunt. Whew, thank God!

30

"With Friends Like This You Don't Need Enemies"

"Fauna!" Will called out to me while I was in the shower.

"Yeah!" I yelled over my music I always played when I was in the shower.

"I'm about to take the girls out for a minute. Hit me up if you leave so I can bump into you."

I could hear the kids running around on the ziggady-boom. Will saved the day because I was just trying to figure out what I was going to do with their bad asses. So with him taking them, I swear it gave me some peace of mind and time to get some business handled. I don't want to sound like I don't enjoy them being around, but hell, every Mother needs a break when it comes to the bambino's. They could be a mess!

"Wooo! Damn that shit felt good!" I yelled out loud nearly bursting my eardrums forgetting about how my voice ricocheted through this big ass bathroom. I was standing in the middle of the floor under the hot ceiling heat lamp rubbing Neutrogena oil over my naked wet body in front of my full-length mirror. As always I loved looking at myself making sho' everything was intact. Being that I was home alone at the time, ain't no telln' what I would do when I was inside my own personal space. I would find myself performing all kinds of dances and acting moves when no one was around. I could be a silly bitch sometimes. Nothing wrong with that! There was plenty of room to do what the fuck ever I wanted to do in my huge ass bathroom tho'. I loved comfort no matter where I was. This was one of the reasons why I had a hard time using other people's bathrooms. If it didn't meet my personal inspection I would hold it until I got home.

At one point this was all a dream. When I was younger, I hoped that one day I would be in a position to have my own place, with this out cold ass bathroom as big as a guest bedroom! Now who said dreams didn't come true? There I was standing dead smack in the middle of my dream. I'm talking about a marble tile stand up shower with the glass doors with 8 showerheads aiming in different directions, which I could control to my comfort. I love being in water. It was a must that Will got that super jet Jacuzzi tub installed to match. It sat directly under a skylight. I swear me and Will would fight over the Jacuzzi, especially after a long trip or day out in the streets.

Every day I prepare for the good, the bad and the ugly, that came with the game I was in. That preparation included being able to relax and get my head right in a warm shower or a few minutes in my Jacuzzi. This was my way of preparing myself for something fucked up in my life to happen. I would always hope I would escape a day of bad karma. I would always take the time out to prepare for the worst, with the hopes of something good coming out of a 16 to 24 hour day. When that day had come and gone, I'd prepare myself to do it all over again the next day. I had a routine.

I know Will had said to hit him up if I had decided to leave, but he should know me by now, that if he got the girls up and running I am open to do what I need to do until Mommy comes back home! If I knew him, he went to visit his Mom's. If he was to try and make an effort to contact me and I don't respond, nine times out of ten he would leave them with his Mom until I returned.

I didn't really get the chance to tell Will about my crazy nightmare after waking me up to some flame-throwers. That weed he had was so toasty I had totally forgotten about everything going on when I woke up! I can't say that it changed the way I felt about my girl Tia, it just made me wonder what the hell the dream was trying to tell my ass! The shit was so fucking real it sent horrible chills through my body! Was this a sign or some shit? I didn't want to hold it against her but I didn't want to disregard the shit either. I'm a play it cool for now and go out tonight and enjoy myself.

I needed something to wear out later to the "office" which was what I called a tittie bar off Hubbell and 8 Mile named All Stars. So I had Tia fall through and roll with me to the mall to find something. The owners changed like wet clothes at this bar, don't know why, but anyone from the hood that knew someone hung out there. All the bad bitches from all over danced there, and all the niggas that was gettin' money conducted business and chilled there.

When I finally met up with Tia she had Robin with her. I was always happy to see them both, but I kinda wanted to have some one-on-one time with Tia to tell her ass about how she bitch slapped me in my dream! From what I've been told about dreams and nightmares you're supposed to reveal them or they may come true or some shit. I guess I would have to wait and see because I never got around to telling her. It just wasn't the right place or time so I threw it out my mind and walked into Somerset mall, which was the go-to spot during this time. If you had money, you had enough to spend at the 'Set'. I grabbed a few new outfits for the girls from Nordstrom and Neiman Marcus.

We were out shopping and messing around for so long, time escaped us. Before I knew it, it was after 8pm and I hadn't heard from Will or the girls and this was kind of strange. Shaking that off, I used that moment of silence to slide my ass back in the crib and grab some personal items to go over to Tia's where we all got dressed.

Pulling up at All Stars that bitch was slappin as usual! Of course we were VIP once we got to the door. The bouncer escorted us to my usual booth, me and my girls ordered up some shit placing a tab a mile long! I was always hungry being that I was a greedy muthafucka, so I ordered us some grub and chopped it up about some other interesting shit we had going on in our lives. I couldn't help the fact that my mind did wander off a couple times thinking about how in the nightmare she set me up, and how real that shit felt. But, not really allowing a nightmare to consume me, I bounced back and enjoyed our moment.

Sitting over by the bar, I stuck out like a sore thumb from my jewels blazing from the florescent lights that beamed down on me. Like I mentioned earlier, All Stars was like the spot where everybody that knew somebody hung out. This particular night was the usual and as always it had a nice crowd. Not too packed, but there were no seats available, so it was standing room only. Being that I was a regular, I of course had no worries when it came to where I sat my phat pretty ass. If someone was sitting in my booth when I walked in, the bouncers and bodyguards didn't hesitate on asking them to move.

Niggas were stopping by speaking and chit-chattin' off and on which had onlookers wondering who the hell we were. It was all eyes on us as usual. Hell, we looked like a million dollars! All the new bitches were throwing all their envious looks our way, mainly because all the balling ass niggas were over there with us! Them hoes probably spent well over $300 between bottles and booths over there looking lonely and deserted. I felt so bad for them that I sent a couple of hungry ass dancers that had been asking us for lap dances over to their booths to entertain their bored looking asses! I paid for everything so them hoes could at least try and enjoy themselves instead of fantasizing on how their lives would have been different if they knew us or better yet, *were* us.

As we sat in our booth admiring the atmosphere, listening to music and watching the freaks get freaked, I noticed a few fellas checking us out! At first I couldn't really read their stares or whether they were ones of admiration or whether they were on that *let's stick them bitches up* tip being that it was so fucking dark! It was kinda crazy because at that point in my life, I knew I had to pay close attention to everything that was going on around me. After all the shit I been through I would be a fool not to pay attention to every damn thing. Sometimes it could be hard for me to determine whether a simple hold of my hand by one of these niggas was innocent and as genuine as a friendly handshake, or if their smile was a frown turned upside down.

What I did know was All Stars had a mixed crowd, which was made up of niggas that was down for you that had their own money and carefree lives, and then you got those hungry hatin' muthafuckas that want what you got and instead of allowing you to school them on how to get their own, they be trying to figure out a way to take it from you! It was one of those nights where the question one would ask themselves was *Does she look like a BADD ASS BITCH, or a QUICK ASS LICK!!* Little did these niggaz know I kept a pink 9mm of my own just in case some shit jumped off!

I wanted my mind to be at ease so that buzz I was aiming for could settle in, and I could enjoy myself a lot more. Rather than be worried about what a nigga may be plottin. So as the drinks kept coming and me and the ladies had our section turnt up, a waitress approached us.

"What would you ladies be drinking tonight? The gentleman over there wants to buy you a bottle." The waitress said in her sexy porn star voice pointing across the way.

I looked over at the gentlemen she was speaking on. He didn't look familiar but shit, when it came to frontin' the bill on some expensive drinks you could be dressed up in a Barney or Big Bird suit and my ass wouldn't care. Hell, spend that shit nigga! I sent her off and running with a long ass tab stamped and addressed to dude with the expectation of some Dom-P needed asap! We had just killed one bottle and were ready for the next!

As we watched the waitress take our bill over to dude's booth we couldn't hold back our laughter as we waited to see what his reaction would be. That would determine what type of dude he was. Within moments after he exchanged hands with the waitress, to our surprise dude passed with flying colors! Now dig this, he not only sent over one but 3 bottles of Dom P! I'm like fuck it I'm a give this nigga the pussy! Naw, I'm just fuckin' around. But, *sheeeit* for a MF to come up out of some bread like that for some women he had never met was instantly attractive!

At first dude caught my interest, now he had my full attention. I can't lie. I was so impressed that I got my ass up and swayed my hips over to his booth joining him and my girl Robin, who happened to be already over there kicking it wit' a dude on his team.

I introduced myself, "How you doing? My name is Fauna." I extended my hand to him. I couldn't help but notice how manicured his nails were and to top it off the Rolex he was rocking had to have at least 100k worth of diamonds in it.

'Now I ain't say'n I'm a Gold-digga... But I ain't messin' wit' no broke nigga...' I silently crooned the lyrics to one of Kanye's songs in my head at the sight of his breathtaking and expensive ass watch! I damn near choked on my drink and I took another sip of it to clear my throat. He matched my fly, but who was he? "I just wanted to come over and thank you for the bottles." I said smiling. He was staring so deep into me that I felt he could read my mind. I didn't like that shit. Don't be trying to read my mind or see my soul nigga. Now I wasn't too sure if I really wanted to know dude. That's when he gently took hold of my hand and smiled back saying,

"No problem beautiful. Anything you want, it's yours."

'Hummmm....' I stared while I was trying to figure him out. He was a very peculiar guy. One that I could see

myself leaning on when Will was on some bullshit. You already know Will ass stayed in the streets fuckin around and I just may have met my next victim.

I swear I been here before, but probably as the biggest male whore that roamed the streets. Over time I started creating some rules to live by, based on my personal experiences and shit. One of Fauna's relationship rules: *Got to have a kickstand to hold my bike up because if I don't, as soon as I let it go it will fall.* That is just a little food for thought.

I continued our conversation after deciding to try and figure dude out. "Wow I didn't realize I had that kind of effect on anyone like that."I teased and we shared a laugh.

He had this look that demanded respect. He really knew what to say to a bitch like me! I had a buzz going so deep I was laughing at shit that wasn't even funny. Shit like how his Mom died and his girl left him. Good thing him and everyone else knew to blame Dom-P's ass for the involuntary giggles.

Before I knew it, our conversation was on point! Good drinks were flowing and weed blowing. That was the kind of shit I loved to be around!! I felt safe around this stranger for some reason, and that was weird as fuck. Especially after that crazy ass nightmare. My attention was so on him that I didn't notice who was standing over me at first until he got my attention.

"Fauna!" A well-known face I hadn't seen in a while tapped me on my shoulder. "What's up Ma?!"

"*Heyyyy* Mack! I'm good what's up with you nigga! Where you been?!" I said smiling and high as fuck.

"I need to holla at you over here for a minute!" The music was so loud it made it hard to understand what he was trying to say at first. He had this anxious look on his face I couldn't really read. Sweat was bubbling up on his forehead as if he had just seen a ghost. I didn't really have a chance to introduce him to everyone at the table by him being so adamant about what he was trying to tell me. I just threw my finger up at him gesturing for him to 'hold up' and turned up my drink slamming the empty glass down on the table.

I noticed the guy who had my attention stare up at us a couple times. I assumed he was trying to see what nigga was pulling me away from what may be the next horse in his stable.

"Hey y'all I'll be right back," I said as I walked away. They ass wasn't paying me no attention anyway. But I could feel the mystery man watching my ass walk away. I later learned his name was Nate.

"What's the deal Mack?" I crossed my arms leaning into him so I could try to hear what he was saying. It was very difficult for him to really go into whatever was on his mind. It was like his attention was being taken away. He kept looking over my shoulder in the direction where I was sitting and over toward the bar where there was a crew of niggas hobbled up appearing to be enjoying the dancers that was all over their dicks. I just wanted to get back to what I was doing and he was really starting to annoy me.

Mack had been MIA for a minute, which threw me off guard to see him at All Stars. To my surprise he kinda went left field on me. I was too damn high to be trying to take in everything he was saying at one time. The nigga was fidgeting and making me kind of nervous. He was

211

rambling on pretty fast about some niggas in the club he heard talking about having me set up!

Now it was something about him mentioning the words 'set up' that had me coming up out of this high pretty fast! I continued to listen closely as he discreetly pointed in the direction of some guys. Now I did notice they were looking over in our direction, but to be able to determine why they were staring and to draw a conclusion from a nigga like Mack who I really hadn't seen in a minute either had me feeling a little apprehensive.

As he went on, I got comfortable enough to let him know that I was good and thanked him for the heads up. I couldn't help but to wonder was there more to the story he was feeding me? Because when I went to walk away he kinda pulled my arm as if he had more to say. I looked at him and asked what was up. He looked around the room again with his mouth wide open like a cat had his tongue, and released his hold on me and then walked off. I guess he saw how anxious I was to get back to that table with homeboy and Robin, and he just kind of backed off.

Hell, I don't know what the fuck he was trying to say so I just brushed it off and made my way over where I was. I ain't gon' lie I was kinda worried! A system filled with drinks and drugs does not help me feel at ease at all. I was even pondering on the idea of whether I should have left right then, or sit my ass back and watch those niggas a little closer. The last thing I remember Mack saying was something about him leaving out and waiting on me in the parking lot with his glock in case something jumped off. I don't know what he was holding back as far as other shit he was trying to say though and that kinda worried me. His attention was taken by something or someone in the room.

But damn, in order for a muthafucka to even hear what he was saying over the loud ass music they would have to be a lip reader or some shit! I was okay wit' his plan to play Captain Save-a-Hoe while I got back over to where I was trying to lock in my next baby daddy. As long as the Pink Panther in my purse was in place that really had a bitch back, I was good.

Don't get me wrong, I kept my eyes pierced on the niggas, *and* on Mack who I watched walk toward the door. I had already made my way back over to where Nate and Robin was when I noticed those muthafuckas he was speaking on follow closely behind him! *Man* I had a bad feeling.

It was like one of those slow rolling scenes in a movie as I watched the unknown unfold. Being the nosey muthafucka I was, I told them I would be right back, and figured I would walk out myself in case of whatever Mack was trying to inform me of. I was sure to get to the bottom of some shit before some shit jumped off!!

He had moved so fast, that by the time I could make my way over to the door he had already made his way outside along with the crew of niggas who I saw head in the same direction! That's when I heard gunshots roaring loud as hell over the music! I was at the door right then with my hand on my shit ready for a battle!

It was so much uproar on the other side of the door! Before I was able to catch wind of what was going on I was being pushed back by some of the bouncers into the kitchen area where I had damn near sprung my ankle and twisted my arm! All types of thoughts were running thru my head.

'*Damn I wonder who got shot…*'
'*What was he trying to tell me, is he ok*'

'Is Robin still with Nate, I hope she got his number for me...'

Pause... Let's go back a year when I first met Mack.

He was this hustling ass nigga that always had shit on the floor, which was how we met through an acquaintance of me and Will's. He had a few chips but nothing major. Like many of the street niggas I knew, he was one of the many that ended up fuckin' wit' some of the dancers that worked for me at my little entertainment gig I would throw every week.

Being one of those ones that wasn't a hater and gave niggas credit when due, Mack had a crazy mouth piece! He could talk a bitch out her draws and a nigga out of some bows if they didn't know what we knew. Slick ass nigga, but was overall cool. Will and I was comfortable with throwing the nigga some work when he was down a few times. Never had any problems as far as him being on top of our bread when it was time to pay up and if we needed him for anything, he was always down.

I remember one time he showed up at an event I had popped off and went for broke on this one red boned/red head chick that tried out for the reality show *Bad Girls Club*! That's how I remembered her so well because she had a loud ass mouth and a phat ass that pulled in numbers every time she performed.

Mack was one of those chocolate ass niggas with a bad attitude that was falling for a hoe that under NO circumstances was about to be locked down with one nigga. It just wasn't going to happen. So this night in particular I don't know if his ass was trying to show off, or if he was just in this jolly ass mood, the way he was just throwing bands at her!

Before the night was over I saw him and her leave together, and that was the last time I saw her. I would inquire about her to see if she was ever coming back to break bread with me and that's when I was hearing in the streets how he was trying to transform this hoe into a housewife. Obviously that wasn't working out too well for either one of them! Word on the street was he was beating the bitch ass so bad she wasn't able to work by her face being so mangled. I wasn't down with that hoe ass shit at all!

One of my sources said he was so insecure with the idea of his woman dancing nude for other niggas that when she refused to listen to him he would beat her straight-face blows to prevent her from doing what she loved. That changed the way I looked at him on a personal level but on the business tip, he was one of the most loyal nigga I've done business with, and that bread was what made me ignore everything else going on around him.

I felt really bad for home-girl but BITCH LEAVE that's how I looked at it! These women get so caught up on that paper they are willing to belittle themselves just to stay afloat. I guess that's the part Mrs. King was trying to school me on. If she were to ask me that question now that I am grown I would tell her that I did not tolerate a lot of shit including a nigga spanking this ass. Well, I do like my ass spanked, but not in the way Mack was setting it off. That's why when I bumped into him that night at All Stars, and was trying to give me a heads up about some niggas trying to get at me I was kind of thrown off.

"Yo Fauna! We need you to chill out in here Ma! Some shit den' went down out in the parking lot!" One of the bouncers confirmed what I had already assumed went down. Somebody's ass got fried.

"Yo D! Go grab Robin and Tia for me!" I yelled out to the bouncer walking away from me heading back out in the bar area.

I didn't know what the hell was going on out in the club! I just wanted my home-girls to be where I was right then until everything settled down.

The next day I woke up sore as hell. My damn ankle and right arm was fucked up from when the bouncer slung my petite frame around, tossing my ass like a piece of bacon into the kitchen area! I knew he didn't mean any harm so there was no need to bring it up to Will.

As far as what happened, just as I had assumed someone did get shot! Though I didn't want to believe who that someone was, it was sad but true, it was Mack. Damn nigga, '*What the hell was that nigga trying to tell me??....*'

Guess that will remain a mystery and I fuckin hate mysteries! I fucking hate these nightmares too.

216

31

"Muthafucka"

He had the baddest bitch in the game wearing his chain and his last name. None of that mattered because Will fucked up major this time! I mean major. I admit my dumb ass stayed around through all the bitches calling both our phones, and the staying out late sometimes, not returning for a couple days. The shit Mrs. King warned me about. I accepted all the excuses. His favorite excuse would have to be he had to go and meet up with some connects, and one thing led to another and before he realized it he was fucked up and had lost track of time. Heard it all before.

I don't know whether I was just overwhelmed by the money he would drop in my lap when he would return or the lavish gifts. He had excellent taste when it came to impressing me. Many called it "Blinded by the bling." I had my own money, but I damn sho' didn't have a problem spending no one else's. The old saying "This was the straw that broke the camel's back", well, yeah… the bitch won't get another chance to fuck over me! I put up with many things but getting another bitch pregnant was something I could not live with. I was down for a lot of shit when it came to the other half. We could get money together, Bonnie and Clyde together and when it came to making that nigga feel like a King in the bedroom… I did that.

But having a baby outside of this marriage, which we *were* married. I had his last name. This was the ultimate disrespect, and he lost that level of respect from me I can't ever see myself bouncing back from.

I realize I been back and forth with this nigga over the years saying many times, 'FUCK HIM I'M NEVER GOING BACK TO HIS HOE ASS!' And what does many of us fucked-up-in-the-moment bitches do? Find our way back dealing with the same bullshit we left their asses for! You want to know what the messed up thing about this was? It wasn't even over no money and his stupid ass decisions he made that ended up fuckin me over many times which *should* have been all the more reason to get the hell on, but it was the money *and* the bitches, the combination was just too much for a Boss Bitch like me. I needed better and I deserved better. All in all, I was tired and it was just time for a fuckin change.

"Fauna! Where you at right now?!" asked Robin.

"At the car wash why?" I responded with excitement being that I hadn't spoke to my bestie since the night of the tragedy up at All Stars.

"I'm on my way up there," Robin said.

"How far are you bitch! I'm almost done and I ain't about to be sitting up here waiting on your slow ass," I asked because she is always so damn slow.

"You gon' want to wait around for this hoe." she said intriguing my curiosity.

The fuck can it be now?

"It must be about some money because that's the only thing my ass would wait around for!" I laughed, but was serious as hell!

"I'm coming," she replied.

We hung up, I lit a blunt and was kickin it with the owner and some of the fellas that was hanging out getting their whips waxed up. I guess many of these street niggas looked at me as one of the fellas being that I had this 'I'm a bout my money' kind of attitude which kept them from coming at me on some sexual shit. I was cool wit' damn near every nigga out in the streets of Detroit that was getting that real paper. I even gave head nods to the little fellas just to make them feel secure. It was something I felt was important to do to minimize the jealousy. Sometimes acknowledging them with a hello or a head nod is enough to make them feel important, and let them know you see they ass. That was my way of thinking at least. You just never knew who had it out for you.

Robin pulled up with someone driving a white Ferrari! I know the expression on my face made gold diggin' reflect on anyone that may have been staring at me. But that muthafuckin car was sharp! Everyone in the car wash had that same look. Though it was a nigga driving that I couldn't make out who he was at the time, dicks got hard and pussy's got wet over that bitch!

"Gawd Damn!" One of the niggas getting his Benz wiped off yelled out.

"Fauna!" Robin blew her horn yelling out her window for me to walk over to her.

I was so into the white ghost I was barely paying her any attention. Unbeknownst to me the person in the Ferrari was following her! You should have saw the envy in my eyes when I saw her ass with this nigga. I'm just keeping it real. Hell, I'm human and though I got mad love for my BFF I still felt some kind of way when I saw that shit. The nigga was whipping the white ghost.

When she stepped out the car and walked over to the guy in the Ferrari I made my way over to them.

"Oh damn HEYYY!" I spoke, trying to remember his name and at the same time surprised to see who the mystery man was driving the $250,000 car!

"What's up Ms. Beautiful Fauna?" He spoke so softly that I had that awe moment where I was damn near speechless.

I hate when I bump into people that know my name and for the life of me I can't remember theirs! That shit is so embarrassing. I held a whole conversation with dude after he had spent over a rack on me and my girls at the club and I couldn't remember his name! Shoot me dead.

"This was why I told yo' ass to wait on me bitch." Robin said under her breath.

We had a sidebar conversation as he took a business call. Now I have never been the groupie type, or the kind of bitch that was impressed by another nigga's shit to have me acting like this! But, I was in total shock when the mystery man was *him*, oh and the ghost he was riding in was the white icing on the cake. I love cake. Anyway, I don't know his name or what his intentions are, but what I do know is I was glad I was looking as good as I was! I never come on 7 Mile without having my shit in order anyways. I knew everything was copasetic.

"How did y'all hook up?" I asked Robin while hittin' the blunt, leaning back on the bumper of her car.

"Girl I had so many damn drinks that night after you disappeared on my ass. Then all the chaos in the club broke out! Niggas came out of nowhere grabbing ole boy up like his bodyguard team taking him the fuck up out of there! Fauna it was some straight Scarface shit." Robin said, She took hold of the blunt and started pulling in that good shit so strong, it damn near sent her to her knees!

"I know that's some good shit ain't it?" I laughed patting her back as she was bent over coughing profusely trying to catch her breath.

"Bitch hurry up and finish telling me before this nigga get off the phone!" I said rushing her. "Okay okay! Hold up!" She held her chest, and gave me the blunt back. "Here bitch! I'm straight on that shit" she said." Because, your lungs got to be immune to that shit to not be on your knees right now," she said in between the tears, choking and coughing. I was cracking up. "Bitch finish the damn story." I said rushing her along ignoring her complaints.

"I was so high that night I couldn't follow everything that was going on, but he asked me for your number. You know me though, I don't just give yo' shit out like that. Plus you weren't around for me to ask. So I gave him mine and he hit me up while I was at the mall. He called asking me to get at you, and here we are."

"You okay hoe?" I asked.

"Yeah I'm good now." She responded in relief.

He was ending his call and walking towards us.

"Oh damn what's dudes name?! I forgot!" I whispered.

"Nate bitch. Your silly as hell." Robin said.

"I'm glad my ass was looking like something. I swear if yo' ass would have popped up on me looking crazy I would have strangled you bitch!" I said jokingly.

"Low key you damn near did strangle me with that strong ass shit you passed me hoe!" Robin laughed but was so serious.

"My bad ladies! Had to take that call. So Fauna, this one of your hangouts?" He said with his sultry but nerdy voice

"You can say that. I'm one of those that never leave the hood." I replied.

"I feel you and respect you for that. I wish I felt the same. I had so many issues with jealous ass niggas out here that I had to leave my hood and finish making my money. I wanted to feed my people and keep them working but they made it hard for a brotha. I had to watch my back every time I came to show a nigga some love" he explained.

"I feel you" me and Robin said, shaking our head in agreement.

"I'm gonna let y'all two kick it. I got something I have to do so I will catch up witchu later, Miss Burks," Robin said playfully as she hurried away.

"Damn we giving out last names now bitch!" I said sarcastically.

I gestured to pass him the blunt and he reluctantly received it.

"Oh damn my bad, you don't smoke anymore?" I asked Nate

"Naw I don't want to choke like your girl was just a moment ago. I may have been on the phone but I did see her ass over here gasping for air after hitting that shit. I was going to click over and call the EMS but that would mean calling 911 and I was not about to do that" He laughed.

"Oh you scared", I teased him in a seductive way.

He kept eye contact with me, which I found to be very hypnotizing. The nigga was sexy as hell, and the way his lips were moving as he would from time to time grace his tongue around them fat juicy muthafuckas. We stood

222

out in the street without a care in the world. He was that deal and I wanted to fuck right then right there.

I knew eyes were watching, and I didn't doubt if one of those nosey ass niggas was on the phone with Will right then telling my business! I didn't give a damn though! I was going for mine just like he go for his when he out every damn night.

"What you got up? Can a brotha take you out to eat?" Nate asked bashfully. I replied, "Of course, I'm following you." I responded walking over to my whip and riding off behind him. That was the day that changed my life.

Not only did I meet my potential future husband, he was my insurance that if all fails on my end he had my back. No more lonely nights. I could just go over to his place. It was a breath of fresh air. We would take trips, and spend time in lavish hotel suites having some of the best sex ever. I found myself falling deep for dude. 'Will who?' was what I would ask myself every time his name would come up in a conversation. I was too far gone.

I was very careful about bringing my daughters around him, being that I still had this level of respect for Will. Plus, you just never know. But as far as how I handled my relationship with dude publicly, I didn't give a fuck who knew, I was wide open. Hell, EVERY DOG HAS HIS DAY, that was how I felt if Will found out. Of course that day finally rolled around, and all hell broke loose!

We were out one night downtown and Will happened to be at the same place we were. He tried me, but couldn't really say shit. I guess because the bitch he so-called had gotten pregnant happened to be with him. So you know what his bitch ass did? He walked right by us like he didn't even know who we were. That was smart because if he would have said anything out of line that would have been the first time he would have caught my designer purse upside his damn head. How fucking dare a nigga try some shit like that, when they know damn well they ain't shit! Double C's woulda been imprinted on that nigga forehead.

Of course he couldn't wait until he got to his phone to call and make all kind of idle threats. I just hung up on his ass, and while Nate was driving I leaned over unzipped his jeans and massaged his dick. Once that bitch got hard enough for me to place my lips around it I tried to suck the life out of it! I was going in on it, forcing him to swerve a few times, going 30 in the fast lane. Then he would speed up to a point I had to come up to make sure my life wasn't in danger!

"Do you want me to stop?" I looked at him as I kept massaging his flesh well lubricated courtesy of my mouth.

"Fuck no." He relaxed his head laying it back enough to where he could see what the fuck he was doing.

I remember him pulling over at some dark ass area out in Farmington Hills somewhere. We were only a matter of minutes away from his house but I guess he couldn't wait. I mean, my head game will have a nigga like that, so I totally understood his position. He needed to get it all. No distractions.

"I just need you to finish what you started," he said as he came out of his pants. It was the summertime, which meant sundresses and I was pleased to feel him making his way around to my pussy using what felt like 3 or 4 of his fingers to fuck me with as I allowed his dick to fall down my throat taking him whole into my mouth.

"Mmmmmmm…" I moaned.

He grabbed the back of my head lifting his ass off the seat slowly throwing his dick into my face like he was fuckin it. I took it all in my mouth and I took it well. I knew how to maneuver that shit whereas some inexperienced bitches don't know how to suck a man's dick without their teeth getting in the way. Not ya' girl. I am certified in that department too.

In any relationship I had in the past, I'm quite sure I will always be remembered. I wouldn't doubt if it's my face they see when getting head from the next bitch. That was the kind of effect I had on men. At least that's what I've been told. Me and Nate had been hitting it off for months since that day, and I was really feeling dude, to a point where I found myself with him damn near everyday! There were times when he would have to go off and do his thing which unlike most street niggas I had fucked wit' he was a little more private when it came to his business and connects.

I would try to be nosey when I would be left alone at his crib or when driving one of his cars. He was extremely careful with his shit though, which could be a good thing I guess.

What's that saying; "Never let the right hand know what the left hand is doing?"

This nigga lived by that street law for real. That's the problem now days, these stupid muthafuckas don't respect the rules and the levels to this street shit. Nate had all that shit mastered, I was in love like a muthafucka. So long Will, but damn we still got the girls so I still had to deal with his ass. Me and Will would have to communicate and keep things cool when it came to them no matter what.

I never had any intention whatsoever in taking his role as a father away from him. But when we were not together, we communicated for the sake of the girls and from a distance I was not thinking about his ass at all honestly! So when me and him both ended up being indicted, that brought us back into the same arena with one another!

It took a federal tragedy to bring us back together. I couldn't fuckin believe my eyes when I was confronted with that shit! I really felt my life was going good and now this shit! I had bounced back from financial losses and a failed marriage and now these muthafuckas wanna kick me down. After getting the horrific news I called up my girls and we all tried to make sense of the paperwork that was available to look over. It was so overwhelming, it was a total surprise, immediately I hired an attorney and went from there.

Snitches were coming out of the woodwork on my ass and I honestly felt trapped. I still was pushing this relationship with Nate, which eased my mind during this madness. It was his comfort and support that I needed more than anything in order for me to get through this. I moped for a ½ a second, Nate held me close but I had to shake that shit. I am a boss so I had to put on my big girl panties and figure this shit out!

"Hey Fauna you gon' be available to come with me to court tomorrow?!" Mason asked to make sure I came through for him on the money tip fa real.

I knew what that was about. All that fuckin money he made with me and now I'm paying attorney fees for this bitch ass nigga to keep his mouth shut. I felt obligated to be there for him though. The FEDS were doing everything they could to build this case against me, Will, and other parties involved. I just hated that I ended up in some shit I had very little to do with! Why even mention my damn name. This indictment wasn't even about ME I was just thrown in this BS somehow!

With all that was going on in my life right then having Nate and my girls on my team made me feel like I had a little rope to hold onto. I had a lot of faith and lil hope left inside of me. Well, at least that's what I thought until that very day came that I will never forget for as long as I live.

I'm downtown arranging to meet up with this bitch Mason at the Federal court building where he had to present himself to a hearing to go over his plea agreement. Now, I had already spent well over $30,000 on his attorney fees to ensure me and him was on the same page when it came to what he would say to them about how much he knew about my involvement. I really felt secure that he would stand on his word. The time he was getting I could have done on my head! It was very simple and I wasn't even tripping about the money. I hadn't mentioned to anyone about me attending Mason's hearing, mainly because I didn't want to appear I had anything to worry about. Furthermore, the shit was embarrassing! So there I was waiting on him to come out. I guess he thought I wasn't coming, because I didn't get a chance to talk to him prior, and I was running late, but I made sure I was there. I really don't like to be at this kind of shit because it never has a good ending, but I wanted to be nosey with the hopes of seeing who else may have been on the snitch list. I sat back in a low key corner in the hallway outside the courtroom door dressed in some attire that my own kids, family and friends wouldn't notice me in. Well I'll be damned! Guess who came walking out with the prosecutor? The sight of them was like a punch in my gut as I backed in deeper to the corner so I could possibly hear what they may have been saying!

"So all the evidence you retrieved on Fauna Burks is in the file right?" The prosecutor asked desperately.

"I told you I'm still working on it Chief, I need more time! But she is passing it over to me on a silver platter. Bitch didn't even see it coming." Nate said in a joking manner as him and the prosecutor shared a laugh.

Wow, I was sleeping with enemy. This was some Set It Off Jada Pickett and Blair Underwood type shit.

I couldn't hold back my tears and I muffled my cries. I wanted to run my ass over there and slit his throat with my fingernail file but I would have been looking at first degree murder. I didn't care right then though. I wasn't in a position mentally to think before I reacted. I just wanted him dead!

The prosecutor leaned over to Nate "So tell me this one thing, did you have something to do with that boy over at that bar that was killed? You know the one that saw us out that time and spoke to you."

Nate looked at the prosecutor with that same eye-to-eye contact he had given me that lured me in to believe whatever came out of his mouth and said,

"A Gangster never tells…"

They both walked away and soon as I saw the coast was clear, I made my exit full of rage, hurt, pain and anger. He killed that boy, I know he did. He knew Mack was trying to forewarn me that night at All Stars and he had his goons take him out! I dug deeper into Nate's background because now that I knew his sole purpose was fucking with me, I needed to know what his role was with the FEDS. *Was he a FED? Was he a snitch?*

Either way I felt, I had to keep up my role as his girl. Now that I think back on it, everything makes sense now. His overprotective way he went about the way he did business and everything! There were times he would have to cancel some of our dates because something important would come up. No baby mama drama, no bitches on the side. You rarely see cats that roll like he did with fancy cars, nice clothes, jewelry and dog ass crib out in the hills with very little drama in the streets. Only police live like that, or this dude could have just caught a case and needed a way out and who did he pick to be his fall girl, my dumb ass.

At this point I needed to gather as much information on him as I could. I'm not going to change shit up at all. I'll keep sucking his dick and feeding him this good ass pussy as if he was the last man left on earth. As soon as I can find that small window of opportunity to get up on dude, his role in this situation will determine his fate and mine.

You muthafuckah...

"Coming Soon!!!"

Beautiful Hustle
Confessions of a "D" Girl
PART II
by
Fauna Burks